The Hollywood Style

The Hollywood Style

Text by Arthur Knight
Photographs by Eliot Elisofon

THE MACMILLAN COMPANY
COLLIER-MACMILLAN LTD., LONDON

For Mary Ann—who lived in none of these homes but has lived with them all.—A.K

To Gypsy Rose Lee—Hollywood's best.—E.E.

Published 1969

The Macmillan Company
Collier-Macmillan Canada Ltd., Toronto, Ontario

Library of Congress Catalog Card Number: 69-12942

First Printing

Designed and Produced by Chanticleer Press, Inc.
Layout by Ulrich Ruchti, assisted by Ellen Hsiao
Printed by Amilcare Pizzi, S.p.A., Milan, Italy

Contents

Acknowledgments

While it would be impossible to express adequate thanks to all involved in the preparation of this book, the first acknowledgment must certainly go to those who so generously opened their homes to us, put up with the inconveniences of lights and cameras, and then spent additional hours with the author supplying the factual material on which the folio introductions are based. Thanks are also more than due to Rupert Allan, of Allan, Foster, Ingersoll & Weber, and to Richard Guttman and William Feeder, of Rogers, Cowan & Brenner, who frequently eased the path to their more inaccessible clients. We are grateful to King Vidor, who accompanied us on some of our earlier picture-scouting expeditions and who was unfailingly helpful in supplying background information from his vast, firsthand knowledge of Hollywood lore; and to veteran realtor Charles E. Toberman, who not only read critically the historical portions of this book but gave us access to his extensive files of photographs dating back to the turn of the century, when he opened his first real-estate office in Hollywood. Acknowledgment is also due to Mr. Victor Plukas of the Press Relations Department of the Security Pacific National Bank in Los Angeles, who supplied many of the photographs used in the historical sections; and to Mr. Myer Rosen of the News Bureau of the *Los Angeles Times*, who helped us to obtain still more. And a final word of appreciation to Ranger George Jackson, stationed at the Will Rogers State Historic Park, for informational services rendered far above and beyond the call of duty, and to designers Tony Duquette and Peter Shore for their generous assistance on architectural details.

Foreword

Over the years, the movies have furnished America with its nearest equivalent to Europe's royalty. As the motion-picture industry moved west, beginning around 1910, it soon concentrated in Hollywood, a sleepy community surrounded by citrus groves and vineyards to the north and west of Los Angeles. Within a few years the movies transformed Hollywood from an obscure dot on the map into the film capital of the world. Because film has a universal language, pictures can go anywhere; but because Hollywood's movies reflected so well the optimism, the romance, the adventure, and the glamour of America, they won special popularity everywhere. Money poured into the studios from all directions and was showered in golden profusion upon those fortunate artists, shop girls, truck drivers, waitresses, and baggy-pants comics that Fate—and the public—had designated as stars. Producers and directors who may have been furriers, glove salesmen, or track layers only a decade earlier, also shared in this rich reward. Soon the streets leading to the studios were studded with their imported custom-built cars, the first mark of their new affluence. And soon, along the eucalyptus-lined avenues of Hollywood, Los Feliz, Whitley Heights, and even as far west as Beverly Hills, vast, opulent mansions appeared, appropriate Valhallas for this new breed of gods. Traditionally, these should have been monuments to *nouveau-riche* bad taste—and, indeed, many of them were, with their ormolu gewgaws, cut-velvet hangings, overstuffed furniture, and profusions of potted plants. But also, simply because their owners had the money and, often, the imagination to give full rein to their own needs and desires, these houses came more and more to reflect the personalities and idiosyncrasies of the men and women who built them.

Originally, this book was conceived to deal only with the Golden Age of Hollywood—Hollywood in the first flush of the opulent Twenties. We soon discovered, however, that the phenomenon was by no means confined to that era, and that the homes of the Thirties, the Forties, and even the Sixties were often as rich and unique as those of the earlier period. That is why this book contains not only the De Mille house but also George

Cukor's, not only Pickfair, the palatial home built by Mary Pickford and Douglas Fairbanks, but also the no less palatial homes built by William Goetz and Charlton Heston in the Forties and the Sixties. Since a good deal of Hollywood's constant round of entertaining takes place in its famed hotels, we have also seen fit to include glimpses of these—including the renowned Cocoanut Grove of the Ambassador. As Edith Head has observed, perhaps no other well-to-do community in the world presents such a wide variety of architectural styles and interior decor as the homes of Hollywood, an expression of both the individuality and the creative urges of those who live there. It is this combination that, we hope, will give this book its special flavor.

We were originally concerned with two kinds of homes: those few, such as Pickfair, that are still occupied by their original inhabitants; and those, such as Pamela Mason's, that had been built by a Hollywood personality (in this instance, Buster Keaton), but which remained, as it were, in show biz. To these we soon added a third category: the homes of producers, directors, writers, and stars of today that reflect the growing taste for art, graciousness, and outdoor living now typical of this community. Probably no other city in the United States, including New York, has a higher concentration of great art in its private homes, nor more homes designed and built by the foremost American architects, from Wright and Neutra to Beckett and Pereira.

Of necessity, we had to be selective. For one reason or another—illness, refurbishing, reluctance—some of the houses we would like to have included were closed to us. Other historic showplaces had been remodeled to such a degree that there was small point in including them. And in some instances the houses had been leveled or dismantled beyond recognition. We shall never forget the afternoon when, with King Vidor, we visited the old Marion Davies mansion behind the Beverly Hills Hotel. The place was swarming with workmen. Its rolling lawns were already denuded of plantings and trees; inside, its new owner had completely stripped away the paneled oak from the huge dining room and from the galleried two-story library that also served (more often, one suspects) as a projection room. There was literally nothing to photograph.

In a sense, therefore, this book is an historical document—the record of a way of life made possible by the movies. By a simple reversal this book may also provide some useful insights into the nature of the American film itself, for the people who live (or lived) in these houses are among those who most influenced and shaped this pervasive art form. Read either way, it is a book to be enjoyed; and we offer it with a word of special gratitude to those who opened their homes to us and made it possible.

I

The Golden Years

I
N 1907, when Colonel William Selig sent a location company to California to shoot exteriors for his *Count of Monte Cristo*, there was little to suggest that within ten years movie-making would become one of that state's major industries, much less that Hollywood—a tiny (population 3,500), countrylike village founded by Horace M. Wilcox, a Kansas prohibitionist—would burgeon into the film capital of the world. At that time production was centered in New York City, with a scattering of studios in Philadelphia and Chicago, all of them turning out brief ten-minute pictures for the wildly expanding nickelodeon market. But as the nickelodeons grew, so did the competition. Many of the new firms entering the field operated with illegal, pirated equipment; since the original companies, such as Edison and Biograph, had patented their cameras and refused to sell them, their would-be competitors had little choice but to import or build machines that infringed on these patents. In a move designed to freeze out these parvenus, the Motion Picture Patents Company, a trust in the fullest Teddy Rooseveltian sense of the word, was formed in January of 1909. Its aim was simple: By pooling their basic patents and licensing projection equipment to theater owners who would agree to show only their films, the members hoped to drive all the upstart interlopers out of the field by fair means or foul. Fair means included court orders and injunctions; foul included goon squads that smashed the illegal cameras and pummeled their operators. Within the year most of the new, independent producers began to beat a discreet withdrawal from New York and its environs. Some withdrew as far as California.

Los Angeles was not the only destination of these latter-day pioneers. "Broncho Billy" Anderson, for example, established his Essanay Studio at Niles, across the bay from San Francisco. But Essanay was a member of the trust; what Los Angeles offered to those who were not members, in addition to its incredibly variegated scenery, was convenient access to the Mexican border whenever sheriffs or the Motion Picture Patents Company agents became too inquisitive. In those free-wheeling days it was not at all unusual for an outfit to toss its assets into the back seat of a car and streak off to Tijuana until the danger had passed. This little convenience had a great deal to do with turning southern California, rather than San Francisco, into a film-production center.

But more than that, there was the climate. Los Angeles has long boasted that the sun shines an average of 334 days a year, with the average daytime temperature a salubrious 71.2 degrees. To the early film companies, which set up their painted flats on open-air stages, this was an unmixed blessing. Also prized was the fact that within a few hours' drive there were mountains, lakes, forests, deserts, orange groves, Spanish missions, picturesque adobe huts, and the Pacific Ocean flanked by a choice of sandy beaches or rocky crags. In January 1910 the Biograph Company dispatched D. W. Griffith to Los Angeles, along with such actors as Mary Pickford and Henry B. Walthall, to take full advantage of these scenic wonders. Griffith promptly set up a small studio in a vacant car-barn on the south side of the city—the first of three he was to establish to escape the wintry blasts of New York. Bison, an independent firm headed by Fred Balshofer, had arrived a few months earlier, also expecting to stay on only through the winter months; unlike Biograph, Bison never moved back.

Although pictures were being shot on the streets of Hollywood in those early years, most of the small studios that began springing up in rented barns or vacant lots either clustered in downtown Los Angeles or moved out to the picturesque hills of Glendale and Edendale or close to the Pacific, at Long Beach and Santa Monica. Not until the fall of 1911, when William and David Horsley opened their Nestor Studio in a former tavern on the corner of Sunset and Gower (later to become famous as "Gower Gulch"), did the movies officially arrive in Hollywood.

Photographs from this period reveal vast stretches of open fields and orange groves in what is now the center of town. Vine Street was flanked by graceful pepper trees, and stately eucalypti lined Prospect Avenue (which after 1910 became Hollywood Boulevard); a red trolley car joined it with downtown Los Angeles, to which, in February 1910, Hollywood had just been annexed. Santa Monica Boulevard, which also had a street-car line, was unpaved west of Gower. For ten cents a trackless trolley with overhead wires carried passengers from Hollywood into the valley beyond through rugged Laurel Canyon; horse-drawn cars performed the same service through the Cahuenga Pass. West of La Brea Avenue lay open fields, and Mary Pickford recalls that as late as the mid-Twenties her then husband, Douglas Fairbanks, would ride across them on horseback from his studio just west of La Brea, on Santa Monica Boulevard, to their Beverly Hills mansion. The center of town was the Hotel Hollywood, at Hollywood Boulevard and Highland Avenue, a rambling structure built in 1903, with additions in 1906 and 1908. (It was here that Griffith and his Biograph crew would break their journey en route from downtown Los Angeles to Chatsworth or the beaches.)

Homes then tended to be small one- and two-story bungalows made of clapboard and shingle, with neat lawns in front and large gardens or even small farms behind. A few more pretentious mansions, such as the E. C. Hurd home at Hollywood and Wilcox, displayed the late nineteenth-century affection for cupolas, porticos, and gingerbread, but combined with a proper Californian regard for open porches and many windows. Wood was still the primary building material, although tan brick was popular for many of the industrial buildings and was used for the new Hollywood High School. Stucco—soon to become dominant—decorated the façade of the Hotel Hollywood and a few of the larger homes.

Curiously, as more of the studios moved to California, Hollywood remained less than hospitable to the new industry, as if fearing an invasion of its placid, semirural way of life. It certainly evinced no regrets when Inceville, with its pioneer shacks and resident band of Indians, arose in Santa Monica at the foot of what is now Sunset Boulevard, nor when Mack Sennett established his knockabout troupe of Keystone clowns in Edendale, a few miles to the east. Carl Laemmle's Imp Company (later Universal) settled in Boyle Heights in East Los Angeles for a time, then moved over the Cahuenga Pass beyond Hollywood to the present site of Universal City. Vitagraph's new West Coast studio was in Santa Monica, Selig's was in Edendale, and Biograph continued to rent space in downtown Los Angeles during its winter hegiras. The meeting place for all these film people was the elegant Alexandria Hotel in Los Angeles itself, which became famous for its "million-dollar rug"—the carpeting in its lobby on which these carpetbaggers from the East discussed, and even on occasion consummated, the fabulous deals that were to bring them all fortunes.

It was one of these encounters that decisively changed the course of Hollywood's history. Robert Brunton, a Scot who had come to this country as stage manager for Sir Henry Irving, had become enamored of the movies and left the company in Los Angeles to strike out on his own. Strolling through Hollywood one day, he discovered a barn owned by Jacob Stern at the intersection of Selma and Vine which seemed to offer possibilities as a studio, and being a designer as well, he sketched plans that embodied his vision. All he needed was the capital.

Meanwhile, back east a new partnership had just been formed by Jesse L. Lasky, Samuel Goldfish (soon to become Samuel Goldwyn), and Arthur Friend to produce a feature-length version of the successful play *The Squaw Man*. As star, they secured the services of Dustin Farnum, who had played the role on the stage; as director, they chose a young man who, although thoroughly experienced in all aspects of theater, had never directed a film in his life: Cecil B. De Mille. The story was laid in Wyoming, but the group originally decided to shoot their picture in Flagstaff, Arizona, because, as De Mille has written, "Arizona was warmer and sunnier than Wyoming." One look at the featureless landscape that lay about Flagstaff, however, was enough to convince them to scurry back onto the train. Its destination just happened to be Los Angeles; and it was there, on the Alexandria's Oriental rug, that Brunton found them and led them to Hollywood.

By the end of 1913, when the Jesse L. Lasky Feature Play Company started production in a portion of Stern's barn, the American motion-picture industry was experiencing pronounced growing pains. Although the power of the Trust had not

An early map of Hollywood (c. 1900) showing planned subdivisions, realtor's residence, and original Hollywood Hotel.

Another good reason why the movies went west—
abundant land in Hollywood at bargain prices.

yet been broken (indeed, De Mille admits that fear of the Trust was one reason for their decision to film *The Squaw Man* in the West), its restrictive force was diminishing as both exhibitors and independent producers defied its edicts. One such edict, for example, decreed that no film could be more than a single reel in length. In 1912 this was advanced to two reels (about twenty minutes), but there the Trust held the line. When that same year a youthful Adolph Zukor imported Sarah Bernhardt's *Queen Elizabeth* from France—in four reels!—Trust officials refused even to discuss with him the possibility of exhibiting it in their affiliated theaters. In desperation, he arranged to show it in a legitimate house, the Lyceum Theatre, on Broadway. So successful was the engagement that Zukor promptly organized his Famous Players Company and proceeded to film, in five reels, such American plays as *The Prisoner of Zenda*, with James K. Hackett, and *Tess of the D'Urbervilles*, with Minnie Maddern Fiske. Meanwhile, in Italy as well as in France, film lengths were increasing even further; an Italian *Quo Vadis?*, for example, eight reels long, had its American premiere—also in a legitimate theater—on April 21, 1913. For those film makers working for Trust studios, however, the rule still held, as D. W. Griffith was soon to discover. During the winter of 1912–1913, once more in Los Angeles, he secretly contrived to film, in four reels, a version of *Judith of Bethulia* in the spectacular Italian manner. Far from being grateful, his outraged employers shelved the picture for over a year when he returned east. By the time Biograph released it, Griffith was working elsewhere, and five-reelers had become a commonplace.

Also during this period movies were beginning to outgrow the nickelodeons. For almost a decade they had been primarily a working man's entertainment; the converted stores in which they were shown were located almost exclusively in the poorest neighborhoods. Now this too was beginning to change. Small, comfortable

"The big red car," linking Hollywood with downtown Los Angeles and Santa Monica.

theaters were going up in the suburbs. Legitimate houses were converting to films. With the appearance of such names as the great Bernhardt, the popular James K. Hackett, and the beloved Mrs. Fiske, the movies were acquiring a distinct aura of respectability; they were reaching out toward the middle classes. The longer films, increasingly based on famous plays or novels, considerably helped in this regard. So did the rise of the star system—another instance in which the independents successfully defied the Trust. The Trust had insisted upon the anonymity of its actors and actresses, reasoning—quite accurately, as it transpired—that once their names became famous, they would ask for more money. Players, working under such sobriquets as "The Biograph Girl" or "The Vitagraph Boy," received as little as $5 a day, as much as $40 a week. It was relatively simple for the independents to raid these companies and carry off their more attractive members by promising them not only a little more money but that most cherished dream of all actors—their name in lights.

This small investment paid off handsomely. As audiences learned who their favorites really were, they returned week after week to see them in action on the silver screen. And if, as the Trust predicted, these same actors who only a short time ago had been content with $5 a day were soon demanding $1,000 or even $5,000 a week, the business itself had suddenly expanded so dramatically that the studios could well afford it. Indeed, for names like Chaplin, Pickford, Fairbanks, and William S. Hart, they began frantically outbidding each other. Summing up the change that had come over the industry was the opening, in April 1914, of the first million-dollar theater constructed specifically for motion pictures, Mitchell L. Mark's Strand, on Broadway. The last word in luxury, with crystal chandeliers, deep-pile rugs, and comfortable chairs—almost three thousand of them—it was an overt effort to woo the middle class. And it succeeded beyond all expectations. Within the next few years every city in the nation could boast at least one such flagship house. By 1915 the nickelodeons had completely disappeared.

It was the crest of this wave that De Mille and his cohorts were riding when they made *The Squaw Man*. So eager were the exhibitors for longer pictures that, prodded by salesman Samuel Goldwyn, many actually paid in advance for the privilege of booking it, thus providing much of the $47,000 that it cost to make. With the success of their film, the Lasky Company not only bought Mr. Stern's barn, which they had

Hollywood's first movie studio, originally a saloon, at the corner of Sunset and Gower.

been renting, but the entire block along Vine Street from Selma to Sunset. When Lasky merged with Zukor as part of the giant Paramount amalgam, the barn continued to serve as a shipping room; and when, in the mid-Twenties, the Paramount lot moved to its present location off Melrose Avenue, the barn went with it. The building still stands—a rare sentimental gesture in Hollywood.

The impressive example of *The Squaw Man* vastly accelerated the move not only to the Coast but into Hollywood specifically. Land was both incredibly cheap—a few hundred dollars an acre—and abundant. So was labor. There were bungalows and boarding houses nearby for casts and crews. It was closer to the Pacific and to the mountains than was downtown Los Angeles, and was literally surrounded by farms, vineyards, and citrus groves. Best of all, just a few minutes away, to the north, was that most famous of all location sites, Griffith Park (*not* named after D.W.), with its extraordinary agglomeration of virtually every type of scenery a film-maker could ask for—parks, lakes, forests, mountains, canyons, even a quarry. It was a few years before one of these earlier producers, Abe Stern, made his famous remark, "A rock is a rock, and a tree is a tree. Shoot it in Griffith Park!" But by then the film companies had long been working on his principle. King Vidor, who arrived in Hollywood in 1915, recalls that the biggest problem of shooting in Griffith Park was to find a site where some other company wouldn't inadvertently wander into your camera set-up.

More important, however, was the California sunshine, then smog-free and crystal-clear. Settings could be erected in the open air with little fear that they would be rained out, fogged out, or frozen out. The sun provided all the illumination that was necessary; sheets of muslin were strung on wires across the tops of the outdoor stages to act as diffusers and to eliminate the hazard of shifting shadows, and heavier materials could be laid across these wires to give the effect of night scenes. Now Mutual opened a studio for D.W. Griffith at the corner of Hollywood Boulevard and Sunset; here he was to make both *The Birth of a Nation* and *Intolerance*—and motion-picture history. Vitagraph moved in from Santa Monica to a new, larger plant just a few blocks from Griffith's. (Parts of this studio, considerably enlarged, are still being used by ABC-TV.) Other studios appeared, some of them small fly-by-night organizations, some to grow into giants of the industry. As C. E. Toberman,

The Heart of Hollywood—Hollywood Boulevard and Highland as it looked in 1907.

Hollywood's pioneer realtor (and still active), has observed, "The effect on the city was a mushrooming growth that almost overnight changed this community from the small, 'countrylike place to live'… to a booming industrial city. Lots sold rapidly, in some cases even before the street installations were completed." The movie boom was under way.

During 1915 the pace accelerated, as is vividly demonstrated by the sharp increase in salaries that movie people were demanding—and getting. In 1914, for example, Charlie Chaplin had worked for Sennett at $125 per week; in 1915 he moved to Essanay with a salary of $1,250—and before the year was out he was dickering with Mutual for a new contract that was to bring him, the following year, $10,000 per week. At the start of 1915 Mary Pickford's take-home pay was $2,000 a week; by the end of the year she was demanding $1,000 a day—and in 1916 signed with Artcraft for $10,000 a week, plus half the profits of her pictures. In 1915 the Triangle Corporation (so named because its principle assets were the producer-directors Griffith, Sennett, and Thomas Ince) sought to enhance the prestige and appeal of its pictures by starring in them the leading lights of the Broadway stage—personalities as varied as Sir Herbert Beerbohm Tree, Weber and Fields, DeWolf Hopper, Billie Burke, and Texas Guinan—all of whom were paid top salaries. One of the lesser lights included in the package was a juvenile named Douglas Fairbanks; he got only $2,000 a week.

Even at these princely fees motion pictures were not yet considered wholly respectable. Frank Case, of Hotel Algonquin fame, tells of John Drew's outrage when a movie producer who was stopping at the hotel dared to make him an offer, and of Fairbanks' initial uncertainty about signing the Triangle contract. "Two thousand dollars was very much more than he could possibly hope for in the theater," Case wrote; "moreover, the employment and salary were to be continuous, fifty-two weeks in the year, not for an indefinite season as in the theater. When I pointed out to him that $104,000 was a handsome amount of money, he said, 'I know, but the *movies*!'"

Case, who accompanied Fairbanks to Hollywood on one of his early trips in 1915, has given an impression of it in his *Tales of a Wayward Inn*: "When we arrived in Hollywood I found it a quaint and lovely place. We used to ride horses all over the country

Producer Jesse L. Lasky proudly surveys the barn used for filming The Squaw Man *(c. 1913).*

from Beverly Hills in any direction, cross-country down to the Wilshire district or in the other direction up through the hills. Sometimes there was a dusty road, sometimes no road.... In Hollywood proper there was a small, comfortable hotel, the Hollywood Hotel, where I loved to stay." Actually, by this time the Hollywood Hotel had become the place where all self-exiled New Yorkers loved to stay—at least until they had earned the bribe that had lured them west in the first place (invariably, it was for a filmed version of one of their more successful plays) and could return to their Broadway haunts with a supply of anti-Hollywood lore with which to regale their less-favored cronies. (Notably few of these Broadway stars, some sixty in 1915 alone, remained in Hollywood for more than one picture. Their stage fame carried little weight with dyed-in-the-wool film fans, which may account for some of their sour grapes.) The day of the Hollywood mansion had not yet arrived, however. De Mille and his family rented a small house in Cahuenga Pass, between Hollywood and San Fernando Valley; Mary Pickford shared a bungalow in the heart of Hollywood with her mother and her then husband, Owen Moore; Chaplin lived first at the Los Angeles Athletic Club (at $12 a week), and then in a succession of second-rate hotels. No doubt all of them, despite their new affluence, were haunted by the fear, as Mary Pickford once put it, "that every year might be my last in pictures. I never once thought my popularity was anything but a temporary and freakish phenomenon."

But as time went on and the golden stream that flowed from the box offices of the world into the studios of Hollywood showed no signs of diminishing, at least some of these fears were allayed. As early as 1916 Cecil B. De Mille bought a palatial home in the spacious Los Feliz district (then known as Laughlin Park, just south of Griffith Park); he remained there the rest of his life. Before long he had acquired as a neighbor Charlie Chaplin, who purchased the house next door. Fairbanks, before his marriage to Mary Pickford in 1919, moved into a great stone edifice in Beverly Hills known as Grayhall (now the home of actor George Hamilton), not far from where the two of them were later to build their Pickfair. Hollywood, Whitley Heights, Los Feliz, Beverly Hills... the pioneers were turning into settlers; and Hollywood was fast becoming a synonym for all American picture-making.

An open-air stage in the Famous Players–Lasky studio (c. 1915). Reflectors provide illumination.

What hastened the process, what actually completed it, was the United States' entry into World War I. When war broke out in Europe, shortages of coal and electricity—plus the fact that cellulose, the film base, was suddenly vitally needed for high explosives—forced virtually all the European studios to shut down. It also added, not coincidentally, to the growing prosperity of the American industry: Europe's film studios may have ceased to function, but this did not reduce the European's craving for wartime entertainment. Hollywood's films and Hollywood's stars brought the war-torn nations of Europe the enchantment, the excitement, the glamour, and the release they so desperately needed; and Hollywood's coffers expanded accordingly. When the war reached America in 1917, the studios in the East were immediately afflicted by the same shortages of coal and electricity as their European *confrères* had been; but for the Americans there was an easy and obvious way out—Hollywood. The studios in New York and in Fort Lee, just across the Hudson in New Jersey, simply shut up shop and moved west. (Many of them already had West Coast affiliates in any case.) New York, because of its proximity to the world of the theater, was able to resume production once the war was over; Fort Lee remains a kind of ghost town to this day.

Hollywood, the community, was not altogether enchanted by this eastern invasion. Reflecting the Midwest origins and Baptist upbringing of many of the original settlers, entertainment was looked upon as sinful—and the movies especially so. As trainloads of film people poured in, signs began to appear: "No Dogs or Actors Allowed." But it was a futile gesture, a last-ditch stand. The movie colony had arrived and, in effect, taken over. By 1918 Hollywood had become firmly, irrevocably, the movie capital of the world. And the decade ahead did more than merely consolidate this position. It turned it into a legend.

For some, the Twenties will always be Hollywood's Golden Era. It was not only the money, which showered down on the chosen few with a profusion that turned many a head and precipitated many a tragedy; there was also an infectious optimism, a feeling that the sun would always shine (in both the literal and the literary sense), which was manifest in every aspect of the film colony's daily life. Its motorcars—generally imported and frequently custom-made—were larger, longer, sleeker, and far more colorful than anybody else's. Rudolph Valentino's cream-colored Mercedes-Benz sported a specially designed silver cobra for a radiator cap. Clara Bow tootled around town in a flaming-red Kissel that complemented the color of her hair, as did the half dozen or so chow dogs that invariably accompanied her. Ralph Forbes's Cadillac included a built-in dressing table; and, despite Prohibition, any number of others contained built-in bars. Parties and premieres were a way of showing off the latest designs whipped up for the stars by their couturiers in New York and Paris. But most of all, their houses provided the most opulent and convincing demonstrations of the film colony's new-found affluence. Often constructed in a style that Dorothy Parker once devastatingly described as "early marzipan," they betrayed all too accurately the tastes and aspirations of their *nouveau-riche* occupants—but were the cynosures of the shining eyes of all their myriad fans who gaped at them in the pages of *Photoplay* and *Picture Play* and dreamed of the day when they might ascend to similar elegance and luxury.

During the early Twenties Hollywood was deluged by literally thousands of girls who arrived each year to turn those dreams into reality. Fed by fan-magazine stories of actresses who had been "discovered" while sipping a soda or waiting for a streetcar, lured by the advertising of unscrupulous talent schools that promised fame and fortune to anyone taking their courses, brought as winners of dubious beauty contests that proffered the inevitable "screen test" as grand prize, these pitiable creatures swarmed into the movie capital armed with confidence and hope—confidence in their own beauty and appeal, hope for that one big break that would make them the next Clara Bow or Gloria Swanson. For most of them the story was heartbreak; for many it was tragedy. Unaccustomed prosperity had proved too heady an experience for some in the upper echelons of the film industry, and stories of wild drinking parties and all-night orgies began to break in the newspapers. The participants were often these same small-town girls who had joined the festivities expecting to meet a producer and win that precious first chance. Others, unqualified or unwilling to find jobs as secretaries or waitresses, drifted into prostitution. By 1923 the

A Hollywood landmark for over half a century—the famed Hollywood Hotel as it looked in 1915.

A decade of expansion: Thomas Ince's (later Metro-Goldwyn-Mayer's) Culver City studio in 1922.

industry itself began an earnest campaign—including the production of a movie titled *Hollywood*—to urge these aspirants to stay home.

The campaign was inspired, at least in part, by an ugly series of scandals which made the front pages in 1921 and 1922. On Labor Day, 1921, "Fatty" Arbuckle, to celebrate the completion of a picture, hosted a party in his rooms at the St. Francis Hotel in San Francisco during the course of which a bit player, Virginia Rappe, was seriously injured and died a few days later. Although Arbuckle was cleared of all charges after three trials by jury, the case was headlined throughout the country, always with the implication that the movie people to a man were drunken, depraved, and debauched. While Arbuckle's third trial was still in progress came news of the murder, still unsolved, of director William Desmond Taylor. What made Taylor's case particularly intriguing were the facts that he had been visited shortly before his death by comedienne Mabel Normand, that among his possessions were found lingerie and letters from baby-faced screen star Mary Miles Minter, and that there was, at the very least, evidence that he knew something about the growing traffic in drugs in Hollywood. Hardly had the excitement over Taylor subsided when handsome Wallace Reid, a top movie idol of the time, collapsed from overuse of drugs and alcohol. These revelations, coming as they did one on the heels of the other, gave confirmation to the growing suspicion that Hollywood had become the new Sodom and Gomorrah. The studios, with unprecedented singleness of purpose, joined together for their mutual protection to form the Motion Picture Producers and Distributors Association of America, with Will H. Hays, Presbyterian elder and Postmaster General of the Harding administration, at its head. One of his first demands as "czar" of the industry was the inclusion of a morals clause in all studio contracts: Anyone under contract could be dropped forthwith for immoral conduct, and a blacklist of "unreliables"—people addicted to drink or drugs—was circulated through the lots.

Such excesses apart, however, Hollywood still retained very much of its small-town air, although Spanish-style architecture was rapidly supplanting the traditional wood-frame buildings. Since most studio people worked hard, there was little time or energy left over for living it up. Even after his success in *Four Horsemen of the Apocalypse* and *The Shiek*, Rudolph Valentino's idea of a big night was to walk down from his home in Whitley Heights to Musso-Frank's for dinner, then to catch a movie at the Iris across the street. Chaplin was prized for his abilities at charades, which had become a particularly popular after-dinner pastime in the film colony. Increasingly, the new houses of stars and producers were being equipped with 35 mm projectors; their proud owners would invite a few friends in to watch their own pictures and those of their rivals. Thursday night there was dancing at the Hollywood Hotel; and the Ambassador's Cocoanut Grove, where Abe Lyman's band held forth, was the fashionable place to be seen: When the Academy of Motion Picture Arts and Sciences was established in 1927, the Ambassador naturally became the scene of its annual presentations. Across the street was the Brown Derby, which was actually shaped like a derby; and as the population drifted farther west, the Beverly Hills Hotel, with its gardenful of celebrity-studded bungalows, and the Beverly Wilshire Hotel became important meeting and eating places.

For transplanted New Yorkers and, later, Hollywood's considerable British colony, the most popular and picturesque place to stay was the exotic Garden of Allah on Sunset Boulevard. Built by the distinguished Polish stage and screen star Alla Nazimova as a rural retreat in the early Twenties, when anything west of La Brea was still considered wilderness, it was turned into a hotel in 1926 (although Nazimova continued to live in one of its villas until her death in 1945). A collection of about twenty-five one- and two-story bungalows lay strewn about its irregularly shaped— and inconveniently placed—pool, and the grounds were overrun with lush, tropical trees and shrubs imported from the South Seas. From the start the Garden catered primarily to the international "smart set." Here, as Garden resident Lucius Beebe

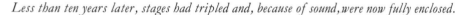

Less than ten years later, stages had tripled and, because of sound, were now fully enclosed.

Looking north from Melrose and Gower—the present site of Paramount's studios—in 1922

once noted, Robert Benchley "presided over the most tumultuous premises I ever saw ... strolling minstrels, twenty-four-hour bar service, everybody welcome, and if the master wasn't in, somebody else was there acting as majordomo." Here comedian Charlie Butterworth, gazing across the pool, uttered his famous "Hmmm, looks like it's going to get drunk out tonight." And here, in the Garden's party room, with an antlered deerskin rug on the floor, most of Hollywood's more festive social functions were held—at least until the film community outgrew its hospitable but restricted quarters. The Garden of Allah was to retain its raffish charm through the Forties, but by the Fifties its never too substantial villas had begun to fall into disrepair and its plant-choked grounds into a jungle; it was torn down late in the decade to make way for the aggressively modern Lytton Savings Building, and its patrons moved a few blocks down Sunset to the more restful charms of the Chateau Marmont.

For the "in" crowd of the Twenties, Pickfair, opened in 1923, became immediately the acknowledged seat of power; an invitation to visit or dine there was roughly the equivalent of an invitation to Buckingham Palace, and the company was frequently as regal and select. No less prized was an invitation to William Randolph Hearst's San Simeon castle, two hundred miles north of Los Angeles; with Marion Davies as hostess, guests were housed in Mediterranean-style villas, dined in a baronial hall surrounded by art treasures from around the world, and traveled by horseback over seemingly endless trails that covered the Hearst estate. On only slightly less baroque a scale was Cecil B. De Mille's Paradise Ranch, where guests were provided with silken Russian tunics, the choicest of food and drink—and, if such was their predilection, the choicest of girls as well. Out in Santa Monica Marion Davies began construction of an elaborate beach house. By 1927, still uncompleted, its cost was $7,000,000. There were ninety guest rooms, a vast terrace, three dining rooms, tennis courts and—only a few yards from the Pacific—a huge swimming pool with an Italian marble bridge that arched across it.

If party-giving and party-going were two of the more popular recreations of the movie colony during the Twenties, the Hollywood premiere was another. Introduced by the popular, diminutive Sid Grauman at his new Egyptian Theater on Hollywood Boulevard in 1922, it proved so successful that when, in 1926, he began construction of his Chinese Theater a few blocks west on the Boulevard, he had its forecourt specifically designed to accommodate the crowds that gathered on these gala occasions. At the grand opening, May 18, 1927, an estimated fifty thousand people were on hand to watch the celebrities arrive for the premiere of Cecil B. De Mille's *The King of Kings*. Culturally, the town was also picking up. The Hollywood Bowl, opened in 1921, gave its first Symphony under the Stars in 1922; it seated fifteen thousand music lovers on crude wooden benches, and the stage and shell were improvised from lumber and canvas. In 1925 the installation was enlarged, the seating made more comfortable, and a permanent steel shell was introduced, as well as the trees and shrubs that today make a visit to the Bowl a delight to the eye as well as to the ear. On May 4, 1926, the El Capitan, Hollywood's first legitimate playhouse—or, as described in the local press, "Hollywood's new temple of the spoken drama"—opened glamorously with *Charlot's Revue*; Gertrude Lawrence, Beatrice Lillie, and Jack Buchanan were the stars. The "spoken drama" persisted for a while, but the house soon capitulated to the "talkies." For many years the El Capitan functioned as the Paramount; more recently it has become known as simply "Loew's on Hollywood Boulevard." The Pilgrimage Theatre began its annual presentations of the Passion Play in 1920; the Greek Theatre, with a broadly diversified program of cultural attractions, opened in 1924. For the athletically inclined there were the Hollywood Country Club, the Wilshire Country Club, the Hollywood Athletic Club and, for auto-racing fans, the Beverly Hills Speedway. Tennis courts marked the lawns of the more affluent, and golf was just beginning to be taken up as a rich man's game; horse racing was then illegal in California.

In 1911, C. E. Toberman reports, Hollywood had one studio and one producer; by 1925 there were 19 studios and 250 producers—and the number continued to grow. But so did the concept of Hollywood. Mr. Toberman, a conscientious real-estate man, had in mind solely those properties that existed within the jagged borders of Hollywood itself—roughly, from Western Avenue to La Cienega Boulevard. But for the movie fans Hollywood by that time was no longer a mere geographical

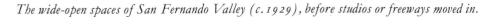

The wide-open spaces of San Fernando Valley (c. 1929), before studios or freeways moved in.

entity. For them Hollywood meant Culver City, Universal City, Burbank—anywhere in southern California that movies were produced. New studios were going up all over the place, and no longer were they simple open-air stages. At first they were large glass-covered sheds that protected the increasingly elaborate settings from the elements. Then in order to control the lighting better, the glass was painted over, and in the midst of California's eternal sunshine electric klieg lights were once more introduced. After the mid-Twenties any new studio—such as Warners' colonnaded manse on Sunset or Paramount's Spanish-grilled *olla podrida* on Marathon—was solidly constructed of wood or masonry and with a lightproof roof. Within a few years these were to be soundproof as well.

Meanwhile, Hollywood was also growing. By 1926 motion pictures had become the sixth largest industry in the United States. A weekly payroll of $2,000,000 gave rise to more and better houses, restaurants, hotels, and department stores. Real-estate values had skyrocketed. A community that numbered 3,500 souls in 1907 had swollen to over 150,000 within twenty years. The movies had come to Hollywood and utterly transformed it. The movies had come to Hollywood and created a new way of life. Something of what it was is reflected in the following pages.

Pickfair, Grayhall, Green Acres

DURING THE TWENTIES, as both the movies and their stars gained in affluence, one mark of this new distinction was the palatial mansions that rose in and around Los Angeles. Perhaps the best known is Pickfair, the spacious home of Mary Pickford and Douglas Fairbanks and, in later years, of Miss Pickford and Charles "Buddy" Rogers. But even before that came Grayhall, begun in 1909 and occupied by Fairbanks while he was courting Miss Pickford; it is now the home of actor George Hamilton. And, most resplendent of all, there is Harold Lloyd's far-flung Green Acres, built late in the Twenties and often called "the last of the great Hollywood houses."

Since the dawn of the Twenties "The White House of Hollywood" has been both literally and figuratively descriptive of Pickfair. At that time Mary and Doug were Hollywood's royal family, beloved of film fans throughout the world and, as part owners of United Artists (with Charlie Chaplin and D. W. Griffith), on an economic par with any industrialist anywhere. An invitation to dine at Pickfair was the equivalent of a royal summons, but it was highly prized in any case; the garden parties that took place on its rolling lawns frequently mingled visiting aristocracy with the movies' most glamorous stars—and it would be impossible to count the number of such affairs that were held for the benefit of Miss Pickford's innumerable charities.

Built by Fairbanks in 1919, Pickfair became their joint residence after their marriage in March 1920. According to Miss Pickford, it was the press that invented the name, although it soon became official; the word is chiseled into a plaque affixed to the marble column flanking the brick-topped driveway that curves abruptly from Pickfair Way to the porte cochère that is the main entrance to the house itself. Immediately to the left of the entryway, opening off a small reception hall, is the Pickfair rumpus room—an elegant version of a Western saloon complete with a gleaming, mirrored mahogany bar that had originally been brought by sailing vessel around Cape Horn, a handsome desk of polished oak which in the 1870's did double duty as a post office, and a scattering of round tables covered with red-and-white-checked cloths. The gray plaster walls are lined with perhaps a dozen original Remingtons, a birthday gift from Mary to Buddy.

A surprisingly narrow stairway leads from the entrance to the main floor above, where at once everything is sunny, graceful, and in quiet good taste. Rich fabrics cover the chairs and sofas, their pastel shades set off by the neutral walls and pale, deep-piled carpeting. Nor are the walls crowded with pictures: The main living room, for example, is dominated by a single large portrait of Miss Pickford herself, painted by Henrique Medina in the early Thirties. A similar austerity is found in the formal dining room, done in a pale powdery green; the room's rich colorations are provided by accents of gold satin drapes and the satins and *petits points* that cover its French Empire chairs. Only the book room—Miss Pickford's favorite—is heavily adorned with pictures, and these are a collection of quietly framed pencil sketches by the sculptor Rodin. Also on the main floor is a small television room *à la japonaise*, with the TV set concealed in a black lacquered cabinet; low chairs with satin cushions are provided for the viewers.

Opening off this floor are wide verandas—another setting for Pickfair entertaining—which give access to broad lawns, a beautifully manicured rose garden, and below these, a king-size swimming pool with an equally king-size pavilion at the far end. Although some of Pickfair's original eighteen acres have been subdivided off, the house stands on the highest rise of the property; from the lawn, on a clear day, one can see all the way to the blue Pacific—and on a *very* clear day, to Catalina Island as well, some twenty-five miles away. A guest wing, shaded by tall trees, extends from the main house on this level; and the Pickfair butler never tires of reciting the endless list of illustrious names—Lord and Lady Louis Mountbatten, King Umberto of Italy, the King and Queen of Siam, Archduke Otto of Austria—who have enjoyed its two luxurious bedrooms and the pleasant sitting room that adjoins them.

The floor above, reached by a wide, carpeted stairway, is devoted to bedrooms and to offices for both Miss Pickford and her boyishly handsome husband since 1937, Charles "Buddy" Rogers. But it is the top floor, known as the Oriental Rooms, that provides the final delight at Pickfair. Here, after a somewhat tortuous climb up narrow, winding stairs, the guest is invited to remove his shoes—Oriental fashion—and enter a veritable museum of mementos picked up by Mary and Doug on one of their many triumphal tours around the world: silken Japanese fans that bear curiously Orientalized versions of their features, kimonos, samurai swords, flags, framed photographs. Cushions are strewn on the rattan mats that cover the floor, and small parties dine here or are served sake. And beyond this room one can glimpse rows and rows of the costumes worn by Mary in the films that made her famous, each garment carefully bagged, camphorated, and preserved against the ravages of time.

But Pickfair, with its priceless antiques and echoes of past glories, is by no means merely a house of yesteryear. Blended with memories of the past are ample evidences of the present. There are, for example, four pianos on the different levels of Pickfair, enabling Buddy, an accomplished musician on a variety of instruments, to keep in practice for everything from rock 'n' roll to the classics. A retired Naval Air Force Commander, Buddy has made many trips with his USO group entertaining troops around the world, as well as making personal appearances for charity benefits.

The entertaining at Pickfair, too, is very much of—and for—the present. It ranges all the way from the annual Christmas party given for blind veterans from the Sawtelle Veterans Hospital (including one 101-year-old veteran of the Spanish-American War) to a musical reception honoring Marian Anderson given by the National Board of Young Audiences to raise funds for the purpose of bringing music to underprivileged children. During World War II Pickfair was famous for the hospitality it extended to GIs passing through Hollywood, with Mary a smiling and gracious hostess.

For almost half a century Pickfair has maintained its eminence among the homes of Hollywood—so much so that one thinks of it neither in terms of past nor present: Pickfair, like Mary Pickford herself, is ageless, a living part of the legend of the movies.

Actually, Pickfair was built on the site originally occupied by the stables of Gray-hall, the second house to be built in Beverly Hills. (Its owner was a retired Boston banker named Lombard, whose other claim to fame was as godfather to Carole.) Douglas Fairbanks purchased the fifty-six–acre estate, still unfinished, in 1919, when he had already begun paying court to Mary Pickford, and promptly converted part of its acreage to the projected Pickfair. After 1920, when Fairbanks moved into Pickfair with his new bride, Grayhall itself passed to Sil Spalding, the mayor of Beverly Hills, who retained it until 1950. The vast ivy-covered building, with a baronial main hall and one of the first swimming pools in Los Angeles, was acquired by the youthful George Hamilton in 1962, who has lived there with his mother, Anne Hamilton Spalding (no relation to the mayor), ever since. Gloria Swanson refers to the multi-roomed mansion as "the Hamilton-Hilton."

Despite the fact that Harold Lloyd's palatial Green Acres spreads over more than sixteen acres, it is all too easy to speed by its single, unpretentious gateway off Benedict Canyon and never even guess it was there. The house itself is reached by a narrow, twisting blacktop road winding uphill through great forests of old trees that provide frequent glimpses of carefully tended gardens, a man-made stream (kept stocked with fish), and artificial waterfalls. At the end of the drive, almost two miles long, one comes upon a vast, fountained motor court—large enough to park dozens of cars—surrounded on three sides by Mr. Lloyd's Italian Renaissance-style, two-story mansion. A graceful colonnade leads to the main entrance.

The house, begun in 1928, when the bespectacled comedian was at the very peak of his career, is built around a rather small, tiled inner courtyard that is used for dining and entertaining. But this inner court is the only small thing about Green Acres. The eastern wing of the mansion projects considerably beyond its basic square design at either end, and a rambling structure that houses the utility rooms and servants' quarters descends from the western wing. (At the height of its opulence, Mr. Lloyd revealed, the estate employed eighteen men for the gardens alone. World War II reduced this number to two, and the higher wage scales of the Fifties and Sixties have held it to eight. The war also eliminated his private nine-hole golf course on the lower acres of the estate.)

On entering the house, one steps directly into an enormous sixty-foot-long main hall, its floors of polished red tile partially concealed by two vast Oriental rugs, its great height accentuated by a wrought-iron chandelier thrusting dozens of tall candles toward the hand-painted wood ceiling. A monumental portrait hangs over an Italian-stone fireplace at one end of the room, and at the other a great flying staircase with wrought-iron balustrades twists up toward the second story. The furniture, though sparse, is appropriately scaled—dark-wooded, heavily carved, massive pieces in the Spanish style. Tall candelabra and virtually life-size statuary further underscore the sense of spaciousness and grandeur: It has all the intimacy of a theatre lobby.

Intimacy, however, was hardly Mr. Lloyd's intent. His thirty-two–room house straddles the Beverly Hills–Los Angeles County line, and he takes great pleasure in explaining that in one of the rooms it is possible to play the piano in Beverly Hills while the listeners are seated in Los Angeles. The main floor includes a formal dining room, a graceful French-style music room, an enormous *galleria* with timbered ceiling and three great arched doorways, and beyond that, an immense drawing room dominated by a hand-hewn stone fireplace that virtually fills an entire wall. The remaining walls are wainscoted in rich walnut, with hand-carved panelings. Oriental rugs lie on the floor; the ceiling is heavily carved and painted in greens, blues, and gold.

But if the interior of Green Acres impresses with its richness and vastness, the exterior delights the eye with its openness and variety. Plants are everywhere—in pots, in tubs, perched high on ornamental columns, twined through trellises, in well-tended cutting beds, in formal gardens, and blooming *au naturel*. The east and border of trees; the west side gives onto a long alley of symmetrically planted roses. North of this rose garden, and reached by twin flights of broad steps that lead down past ivied walls, lies the first of several formal gardens—a beautiful stretch of greensward bordered by flower beds, and also by myriads of potted plants that can be changed with the seasons, thus keeping the area colorful all year round. A large, decorative fountain splashes at the upper end of the garden, and a graceful, colonnaded tea pavilion provides shade at the other end. Off to the left of this garden a narrow path leads to the children's garden, where silhouetted story-book characters man the decorative gates and usher the visitor into a lilliputian world that includes a miniature thatched farmhouse and stable, both completely furnished to scale.

At the east end of the house, roughly paralleling the driveway leading up to it, two Roman columns topped with gargoyles mark the beginning of Green Acres' waterfall garden. Water from a huge stone basin trickles downward through a series of smaller basins that form the centerpiece of a long, cobblestoned corridor framed by Italian cypress and green shrubs, to which urns of flowering plants add sudden splashes of color. Another fountain, centered in a shaded, circular landing paved with a mosaic of colored pebbles, provides the terminus to the twin walkways of this secluded garden. To its left, bordered by pepper trees and weeping willows, lies a calm reflecting pool, its surrounding walk flanked by eight stately urns filled with plants, its surface broken by water lilies and the plashing of fountains near either end. At the far end, beyond a concrete pergola in the Mediterranean style, a low curved wall lined with benches commands an impressive view of the estate.

When Harold Lloyd built his home, it was his custom to train for each picture as intensively as any Olympic athlete, so Green Acres also comes well supplied with recreational facilities: swimming pools, tennis courts, handball courts, and until the Forties, the nine holes of golf. Now in his seventies, Mr. Lloyd has turned to less strenuous hobbies, such as painting and photography. But as he led us over his estate, cameras slung from his shoulders, the spring was still in his step, and as he pointed out one favorite camera set-up after another, there remained all the buoyant enthusiasm of that youthful Harold whom he likes to call "the glasses character."

Through these portals, the gates
to Pickfair, have passed the
royalty not only of Hollywood but
of the entire world.

Overleaf:
Charles "Buddy" Rogers at
Pickfair's Western-saloon—
styled bar. A dozen Remington
originals line the walls.

The formal dining room at Pick-fair (right) presents a scene of quiet elegance, whereas the main living room (below), dominated by a portrait of Mary Pickford, is simple, comfortable, and cozy.

IN THE KISS OF THE SUN THERE IS PARDON
IN THE SONG OF A BIRD THERE IS MIRTH;
WE ARE NEARER GOD'S HEART IN A GARDEN
THAN ANYWHERE ELSE ON EARTH,

At the foot of Pickfair's flower-filled gardens a statue (left) salutes the glories of nature. The guest wing (below), separated from the main house, looks out over the gardens and an Olympic-sized swimming pool.

At the far end of the saloon, a desk of polished oak (left) which doubled as a Western post office in the 1870's. On the top floor of Pickfair, in the Oriental Rooms (below), are the mementos of triumphal worldwide tours of "America's Sweetheart," Mary Pickford, and her equally illustrious husband during the Twenties, Douglas Fairbanks.

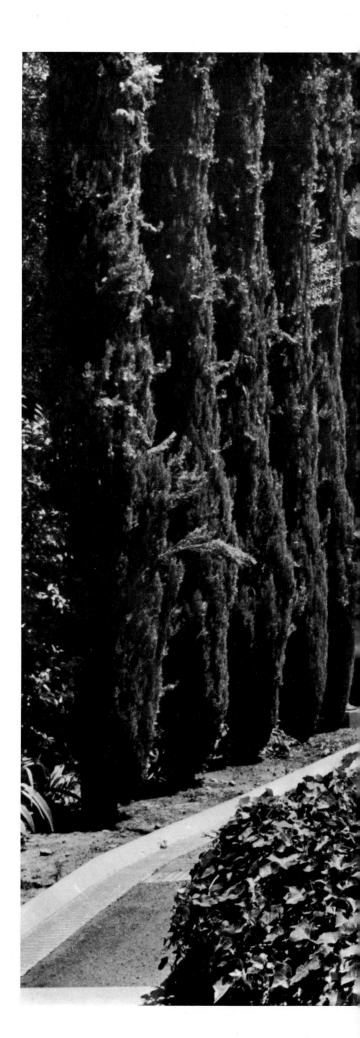

Harold Lloyd's palatial Green
Acres bestrides the Beverly Hills–
Los Angeles County line and
includes forests, a man-made
stream, artificial waterfalls, and
gardens ranging from a Hansel
and Gretel children's garden
(above) to vast tree-shaded
esplanades in the Italian style
(right).

Overleaf:
When Douglas Fairbanks courted Mary Pickford in 1919, he did so from the vast ivy-covered mansion now occupied by the youthful George Hamilton.

Cecil B. De Mille

NE OF THE FIRST of the Hollywood mansions, and by all odds the most permanent, is the home of producer-director Cecil B. De Mille; purchased in 1916, it is still occupied by his daughter, Mrs. Cecilia Harper, and her family. Rambling and comfortable, it stands atop a hill in what is now the Los Feliz district of Los Angeles (formerly Laughlin Park), just south of famed Griffith Park, and north and a little east of Hollywood. This area, predominantly residential, with broad, well-manicured stretches of lawn and great stands of pine, palm, and cypress, was an early favorite of the movie colony, as many of its street signs attest: Cummings Drive, Talmadge Street, and of course, De Mille Drive. The narrow road that winds up to the De Mille estate, incidentally, is sternly marked "Private," and the entry to the house itself is unobtrusive in the extreme—purposely so.

Actually, the De Mille house is two houses, both in the popular Mediterranean style, joined together by a long, red-tiled, door-lined arcade, the inner side giving onto a greenhouse devoted to all varieties of orchids. The larger house, which includes the porticoed main entrance, is the one that De Mille moved into in 1916. Its main floor features a large but simple and homey parlor and an oak-paneled formal dining room with exuberantly carved teak chairs surrounding a long oak table; the second floor provides sleeping quarters for the family. But it is the second house, which De Mille acquired as a guest house in 1919 from his neighbor, Charlie Chaplin, that is obviously the nerve center for the entire establishment. One follows the glassed arcade past several alcoves filled with rare books, bibles, and bibelots to an enormous paneled room dominated by an elaborately carved desk and the pink-patterned highback chair from which the Master ran his affairs. Everything on the desk—the clock, the carved Buddha, the telephone, the worn tooled-leather folder containing letters and documents demanding his attention, the heavy letter opener, the carved magnifying glass—is meticulously arranged, precisely in place. (Even today, a decade after De Mille's death, his secretary turns the calender each day and places a fresh rose in the bud vase on the desk.) Underneath the desk a cluster of four fly-swatters still hangs next to his right knee, ready for instant use; and a Chinese brass opium bowl, some two feet in diameter, remains to catch the ashes from the Master's pipe.

Across the room the wall facing the desk is crowded with plaques and trophies, an impressive reminder of the multiple rewards of De Mille's rich career; below these, in a gilded, pillared book shelf, are leather-bound copies of his numerous scripts and the compiled historical research that went into the writing of them. In front of these, glassed into a wooden reading stand, are carved red-granite replicas of the tablets bearing the Ten Commandments which Moses received. Statuettes, loving cups, and other awards lie strewn with casual ostentation throughout the great beamed hall.

What alters the museumlike atmosphere of this room, however, is a vast, framed VistaVision screen that stands firmly, permanently planted at the far end, concealing the ornate fireplace behind it. In most Hollywood homes the movie screens are generally designed either to disappear neatly into the ceiling when not in use or, at the very least, to roll up and be carted away by the butler until the next séance. Not with De Mille. Obviously, this office stood ready night and day to be transformed into a screening room at a moment's notice, requiring merely the removal of the battered Pathé camera with which he shot the original *Squaw Man*, his first film, in 1913; it stands on a low table directly in front of, and in the center of, the screen. One can only imagine the midnight conferences with harassed writers, the self-congratulatory previews of his latest opus, and the constant viewing of the work of rival producers and directors which took place in this room.

Despite the size of the screen, however, the room is not set up to accommodate great numbers of viewers. A large, Mexican-blanketed divan faces toward it, and several leather or plush-covered armchairs. Behind the divan stand eight or ten canvas director's chairs that could be pulled out for the screenings and set up in front of De Mille's collection of antique pistols and rifles or placed beyond these in the alcove that was the original entryway to the house when Chaplin owned it. At most, no more than two-dozen people could view the screen with any comfort while De Mille himself, ensconced in a leather chair, shied matchsticks at his outsized opium bowl.

"Keeping the same house for four decades must be something of a record in Los Angeles," wrote De Mille in an autobiography published shortly after his death in 1959. "Since I came to California in 1913 I have never lived anywhere but in Hollywood. There I have done my work. There I hope to die; and my last earthly home is waiting for me there, in Hollywood Cemetery." But though his ashes may rest in an imposing mausoleum in that cemetery, the spirit of the man still lives in the cluttered, spacious office just off De Mille Drive.

For pioneer producer-director Cecil B. De Mille, not his home but his office was his castle. He worked surrounded by the awards and trophies of his long career, as well as by the books (below) that documented his religious extravaganzas. Before the screen (right) stands the original camera on which he shot The Squaw Man, *Hollywood's first feature.*

At the end of De Mille Drive
in Los Feliz, the De Mille estate
(above). Apart from the mammoth office, the home is modestly,
unpretentiously furnished—as
evidenced by the quietly comfortable living room (right).

The De Mille house is in fact
two houses, one originally belonging to Charlie Chaplin, connected
by a long glass-enclosed corridor.
On one side is a greenhouse in
which De Mille grew his favorite
orchids.

William S. Hart

OWBOY STAR William S. Hart was reputedly a hard man with a dollar. As a leading figure in the motion picture industry in 1919, he was approached by Charlie Chaplin, Douglas Fairbanks, D.W. Griffith, and Mary Pickford to join them in the formation of United Artists. Hart allowed he was interested—if they would put up his share of the initial capital. Hart never became a United Artist, but he did amass a considerable fortune before his retirement from pictures in 1925, whereupon he devoted the next three years to the construction of his La Loma de los Vientos on the 253-acre Horseshoe Ranch in Newhall which he had purchased in 1920. He continued to live here until his death in 1946, after which, handsomely endowed by Hart himself, the ranch was turned into a Los Angeles County park. "While I was making pictures," he once said, "the public gave me their nickels, dimes and quarters. When I am gone, I want them to have my home." Admission to the park, as stipulated in his will, is free of charge, and the home itself, intact, has become a museum not only of Western lore but also of the American theater. (Between 1889 and 1914, when he entered films, Hart had established himself as an important Shakespearean actor, appearing opposite such stars as Modjeska, Julia Arthur, and Ada Rehan; he also portrayed Messala in the original stage production of *Ben-Hur* in 1899. Mementos from this era are also included in the Hart collection.)

The approach to the house, which is considered to be one of the finest examples of Spanish-Mexican architecture in southern California, is through a long, winding road that leads gradually up to the promontory that Hart chose as his building site. To the left as one drives into the estate stands the original ranch house, built in 1910 (and now filled with memorabilia from Hart's film career); the rolling grounds to the right have been reserved as a picnic area. The road curves past an Olympic-sized swimming pool, then turns abruptly toward the white-stucco, two-story mansion with its Spanish-tiled roof, set in a handsome stand of cypress and pine.

Although all fourteen rooms in the house are filled with relics from Hart's career, perhaps the most impressive of these is the spacious living room, angled off from the main house in a wing of its own. At first glance, it might be the spread of any well-to-do rancher, with its timbered ceiling, overstuffed chairs, and bearskin rug sprawled in front of a generous fireplace. A grand piano tucked in a corner amidst velvet-draped windows, and an outsized radio-phonograph cabinet in the ponderous style of late Twenties-expensive contribute a curiously middle-class note to the room. But then one begins to see the intricate handiwork on the vast, notched crossbeams supporting the ceiling; they are carved and painted in Indian motifs, with heavy, hand-carved corbels. One begins to notice the richly hued Indian weaves that serve as carpeting throughout. And one begins to recognize, among the ornamental saddles, spurs, and vests that adorn the room, that the paintings and sculpture include the work of such noted artists as James Montgomery Flagg, Frederic Remington, and Charles M. Russell. Russell had been a close friend of Hart's until the former's death in 1926, and the Hart collection includes eighteen of his paintings and five of his bronzes.

A great circular stairway, lined with large James Montgomery Flagg illustrations of scenes from the William S. Hart films and books (Hart authored a dozen novels and books of short stories between 1919 and 1940), leads up to the second floor. As in the living room, the supporting beams above the rounded stucco walls have been carved and painted with Indian designs. At the head of the stairs, crouching forward in characteristic pose, stands a life-size bronze of Hart in full cowboy regalia, the work of C. C. Cristadoro; and in the hallway beyond, mounted in display cases, hangs part of his collection of historic firearms.

It is the bedroom, however, that best expresses the essence of the man. Relatively small—indeed, almost Spartan—it has been preserved exactly as it was when Hart died, and actually looks as if it were being kept in readiness for his return. His hand-tooled boots with their silver spurs stand on an Indian rug in the center of the room; his flat, broad-brimmed cowboy hat and a pistol are laid out on a hide-covered chest nearby. The narrow bed with its Indian throw is surmounted by a Hart portrait and pictures of his favorite mounts, and flanking the bed, one night table holds a simple lamp and a few books, the other an inexpensive radio.

Elsewhere on the grounds other buildings—a bunkhouse, a barn, a white-fenced corral—capture the look and feeling of that frontier West that William S. Hart knew and loved because he had grown up in it. It was in tribute to Hart and to that earlier way of life that in 1962 Walt Disney donated eight buffalo to the park, the first in a herd that has now become a highpoint in any visit to the Hart estate.

*Typifying the world of cowboy
star William S. Hart is his
unique collection of authentic
Western "shooting irons," prominently displayed in his former
ranch home, now a museum. His
bedroom (below, right) is arranged
as he would have left it. At the
head of the stairs a life-size
bronze by C.C. Cristadoro (far
right) captures a characteristic
gesture.*

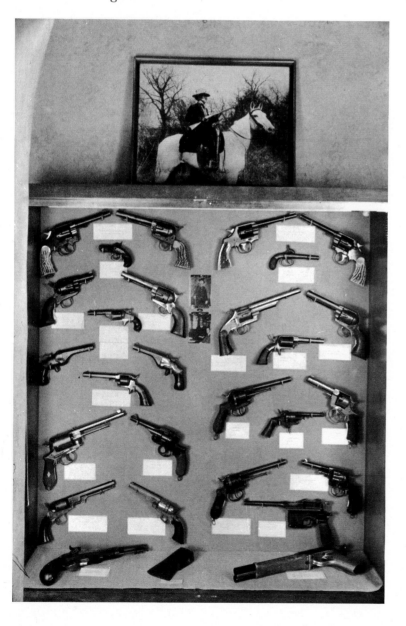

The William S. Hart home in
Newhall (right), an outstanding
example of Spanish-American
architecture.

The living room of the Hart ranch (left)—a mixture of middle-class comforts and Western-style elegance, graced with silver-studded saddles and Charles Russell bronzes. The stairway (below) is hung with illustrations by James Montgomery Flagg of Western scenes from Hart books and films.

Tony Curtis
Pamela Mason

URING THE TWENTIES, Beverly Hills became the mecca for the movie colony, attracted there by the proximity of such notables as Mary Pickford and Douglas Fairbanks and by the special tax concessions afforded by the Beverly Hills authorities. New wealth (and low income taxes) encouraged the construction of virtual palaces on multiacred estates. Among the more palatial were the Mediterranean-style villa that film producer Joseph M. Schenck built early in the Twenties for his beautiful wife, Norma Talmadge, and the Italian villa that the great frozen-faced comedian Buster Keaton built in 1925 for *his* beautiful wife, Natalie, the sister of Norma. Since 1967, the Schenck house has been owned by actor Tony Curtis, while the James Masons have had the Keaton house for over twenty years. (Since their divorce, it has been occupied by Pamela Mason and their children, Portland and Morgan.)

Electronically controlled iron gates bar the unwelcome visitor from the almost five acres that surround Tony Curtis's home; beyond the gates, a wide, curving driveway leads through meticulously tended lawns to a tan, two-story mansion with terra-cotta tiled roof. Inside the house, one steps almost immediately into a vast reception hall, which, like all but one of the rooms on the main floor, is paneled with warm, polished woods. A broad wooden stairwell, open to the entire height of the house, leads to the bedrooms and a sitting room above. Off the reception hall a wide passageway, also paneled, gives access to the other rooms on the main floor, with a large dining room at one end and a vast living room at the other.

Curtis takes justifiable pride in the fact that the furnishings—most of which look as if they might have come with the house, so snugly do they fit into its style and dimensions—are actually his own. Many of them, such as a twenty-foot dinner table fashioned from a single plank, he purchased years ago and stored against the day that he would have a suitable place in which to display them properly. He takes equal pride in the growing collection of paintings and lithographs that line his walls, most of them by such contemporary artists as Brigitte Riley, Jan Stussy and Andy Warhol. (He has also been particularly fortunate in his selection of works by the more venerable painters: An unauthenticated Picasso that he bought some years ago was recently scrutinized, then signed by the Master; and when a Braque that he had acquired showed signs of scaling, he took it to a restorer, who uncovered an entirely different—and superb—painting on the reverse side. Two Braques for the price of one!)

But Curtis's greatest joy, because they have come to mean so much to him personally, is his extensive collection of boxes by the Surrealist artist Joseph Cornell, boxes filled with adroitly maneuvered and imaginatively juxtaposed bits of art and artifact. Cornell's work so impressed Curtis that he began to build boxes of his own —not as a hobby but as an eminently satisfying form of creative expression. Many of these are prominently displayed in a large, blue-lined armoire that dominates one end of the living room, while others stand in the hallway of his comfortable den. As with most of the art in his house, he moves them frequently lest their edge grow dulled by overfamiliarity.

The one exception to this are the six large Surrealist paintings by Jan Stussy that line the curving walls of Tony Curtis's sunny breakfast room (which, incidentally, is also the only downstairs room that is not wood-paneled). Curtis himself refers to it as his "Stussy room," and delights in the fact that he acquired the canvasses well before the artist's reputation was established by gallery and museum exhibitions. The circular room gives on a broad stone terrace that looks out to a section of the wall surrounding the estate, topped at regular intervals by the potted *bonsai* trees that are his special favorites. Curiously, in the midst of all this opulence, Curtis and his wife live quite modestly with one housekeeper and a gardener. Only the affection that Curtis openly displays for his house is lavish.

By one of those neat Hollywood coincidences, not only was Pamela Mason's home originally occupied by Joseph Schenck's brother-in-law, but during World War II the Schenck house provided a refuge for Mrs. Mason's stepmother, the famed English beauty Marjorie Ostrer. When the Masons acquired the Keaton property shortly after the war (for $80,000, although it had cost Keaton over $300,000 to build), it still included a vast terraced slope with some sixty marble steps leading down through a cypress alley to a huge swimming pool below. Taxes forced the Masons to sheer away this extravaganza and subdivide the lower section into three lots; but the house above, apart from the addition of a new swimming pool and tennis court, stands substantially as it was in Keaton's day—a white stucco, two-story building whose generous wings enclose on three sides a wide flagstoned patio.

"It took a lot of pratfalls to build *this* dump," Keaton used to say—and one can believe him. A number of small salons, one of them now an office, open off the terra-cotta-tiled entryway. Arched corridors lead to a banquet hall, a library, a black and white marble-tiled *lanai*, and to a combination living room–projection room with a high beamed ceiling. ("One reason that so many movie people today buy former movie stars' homes is that they were the only ones who could afford projection equipment," Pamela Mason observes. The Masons' only addition to it was a Cinemascope screen when the new process outmoded the original "postage stamp" screen. They also painted out the figures of cupids pursuing each other with darts that had formerly adorned the ceiling, and moved the bar out of a cupboard into the room itself.) Five bedrooms upstairs, a small guest house and a three-car garage flanking a huge circular motor court complete the property.

Much of the art in the house consists of pictures done by James Mason (almost an entire wall in the living room is covered with caricatures that Mason drew of himself), by their talented children (Fred Allen once called a finger painting by Portland that hangs framed over the library door "a hemorrhage run rampant"), or by their numerous friends. An ardent ailurophile, Mrs. Mason has a collection of twenty cats, all of them strays, which she provides with their own "cat room" on the main floor. Her two dogs, on the other hand, are left to fend for themselves. With her own warmth and personality, Pamela Mason has managed to convert what might easily have been a white elephant into a singularly snug and happy abode.

Surrounded by the luxury of another day (his home belonged to former film-tycoon Joseph M. Schenck) and the most emphatically modern of mod and op art, actor-producer Tony Curtis typifies the continuity to be found in many movie-colony homes. Not typical, however, are the small jewel-like boxes (above, right) that Curtis makes himself and gives or sells to friends—nor the impressive collection of Stussy canvases that adorn his sunny breakfast room (left).

Also emphasizing this continuity is the palatial home of Pamela Mason, once the property of comedian Buster Keaton. The living room (below), which is also a game room, comes equipped with projectors; the screen lowers automatically behind Mrs. Mason and friends (including Zsa Zsa Gabor and Tony Aquaviva, with cue). The jazz combo performing in the black-and-white–marble lanai *(right) was put together by son Morgan, who plays electric guitar.*

Jennifer Jones

ONE OF THE most handsome, and historic, homes in Beverly Hills is the white-stucco, Spanish-style mansion of Jennifer Jones, widow of the late David O. Selznick. Adjacent to the John Barrymore estate, which was first owned by King Vidor, it was built in 1925 by screen star John Gilbert, who wanted to be near Vidor, his close friend and favorite director. For a time the two men had the hilltop completely to themselves—apart from the various lights of love which the romantic Gilbert kept escorting up winding Tower Road. It was here that he wooed the elusive Greta Garbo (who learned tennis on the Gilbert court under Vidor's tutelage). After Vidor sold his property to Barrymore, Gilbert stayed on with his first wife, Ina Claire, and then with his second, the beautiful Virginia Bruce. Later, Miriam Hopkins acquired the estate, and after her the Selznicks, whereupon it promptly became one of the most popular centers for social gatherings in the entire movie colony.

Nothing could be less pretentious than the entrance to the estate. The road widens slightly to permit parking opposite the house, and from a small wrought-iron gate a narrow path leads upward through a well-tended garden to a modest patio entryway. Beyond the house, which is surrounded with palms, oaks, and eucalypti, lie the tennis courts and swimming pool; and beyond these, on the highest point of the property, stands a huge green water-tower that is visible for miles.

But if the low, irregularly shaped exterior, with its Spanish-tiled roof and turret, suggests simplicity and isolation, the sumptuous interiors, completely redecorated for Miss Jones since the death of her husband in 1965, quickly dispel any such illusion. As designed by Tony Duquette, one of Hollywood's most fashionable decorators, the main drawing room picks up its mellow tones from a beamed, wooden ceiling. The walls, repeatedly broken by tall, built-in bookshelves, are covered in a beige linen burlap. The eye is immediately drawn to an ancient Chinese scroll painting of great quality above the fireplace, and before it, in the very center of the room, stands a large coffee table topped in travertine. Japanese screens from the Momoyama period and a beautiful antique Chinese rug in imperial yellow add grace and lightness to the room. Drawings by Renoir and Augustus John, as well as a splendid Graeco-Roman torso in bronze, lend it their own special elegance.

Because Jennifer Jones had always claimed she wanted a "gypsy room," Duquette designed the master bedroom with this wish in mind. The room, a later addition to the house, was literally tunneled out of the rock foundation on which it stands, and hence looks out directly on the gardens and an ornamental fountain—a view reflected in the giant mirror that hangs behind the bed. Indian saris curtain the picture window, and a carved Indian angel stands guard nearby. On the opposite side of the room, in a recessed nook with a built-in divan and bookshelves, hangs a rich seventeenth-century Indian embroidery; the vast bed that dominates the room has a cushioned headboard and throw in amethyst, pink, red, and fuchsia which have also been fashioned from antique Indian embroideries. To the left of the bed hangs a large Siamese wood carving, a traditional charm to ward off evil spirits, and near the foot of the bed, against the aubergine walls, stands a large Siamese Buddha in full panoplied robes. It is clearly the bedroom of a very happy "gypsy."

In addition to the bedroom, and also carved from the hill, Miss Jones's suite includes a sitting room, a huge clothes closet, and a handsome wood-paneled bath. (Mr. Duquette acquired the *boiserie* for the bath from playwright Zoë Akins and accented it with large oval and upright mirrors and a graceful crystal chandelier. Above the recessed tub hang four framed Renoir sketches.) Nearby is the bedroom of Miss Jones's daughter, Mary Jennifer, its style set by the canopied four-poster bed with flower-bordered drapes and pillow covers printed in France. Continuing the French note are the porcelain chandelier and the fretted sliding screens fitted into the alcove window.

Over the years there have been numerous additions to the Selznick house: open balconies enclosed and converted into sun-drenched sitting rooms, excavations to provide additional space, and redecorations that never seem to end (except for the room that once served as an office for David Selznick, with its portrait of Jennifer Jones over the recessed, carved-wood fireplace—perhaps as a memorial to him, this room remains virtually intact). With all the changes, however, the house remains essentially what it always was—patrician in its elegance, intimate and personal in its warmth.

Built in 1925 by silent-screen
star John Gilbert, the Jennifer
Jones (Mrs. David O. Selznick)
house looks simple and unpretentious on the outside, but the
interior—designed by Tony
Duquette—is rich and tasteful, as
the paneled living room (below)
eloquently attests.

Overleaf:
Jennifer Jones's "gypsy room"—
a bedroom mingling Indian and
Siamese motifs, with garden and
fountain glimpsed through a
picture window and reflected
from a mirror behind the bed.
Antique Indian embroideries
line the recessed reading nook
(A) in one corner of the bedroom. The bath (B-C) has been
fitted with elegant polished
woods, including a desklike
dressing table. Daughter Mary
Jennifer's room (D) is made
fresh and youthful by flower-
bordered draperies (printed in
France) on the four-poster bed
and at the windows.

A

B

C

D

John Barrymore

"T HE HOUSE was a castle out of Fairyland, hanging from the crest of a precipitous mountain. Actually it was a little village, a hacienda of half-a-dozen buildings with red tiled roofs, iron-grilled windows, and gardens." Thus does Diana Barrymore describe her first impression of her famous father's hilltop estate when she visited it early in 1942. Already time—and the creditors—had begun their ravages upon its sprawling interior, where once the wits, the literati, and the intelligentsia of the movie colony had gathered in noisy profusion. Many of the rooms had been sealed, their furnishings sold off. "The library, with foot-thick doors," Miss Barrymore reported, "looked like a dusty attic."

Happily, this vast, sprawling fifty-two–room mansion, with its two swimming pools, trout pond, tennis courts, and bowling green, has not only been saved from the subdividers but in large measure restored to its former opulence through the industry and affection of its present owners, Mr. and Mrs. Hugo Grimaldi. Mr. Grimaldi is a motion-picture director–producer and a direct descendant of one of the oldest and most aristocratic families in Europe.

The six-acre property, with its view of the distant Pacific, first belonged to director King Vidor. In 1924 Vidor built on it a hacienda with pool and tennis court which became the nucleus of the Barrymore additions. Barrymore acquired it from Vidor while he was ardently courting the beautiful Dolores Costello, who became his third wife in 1929. A symbol of this courtship appears in a Tiffany glass window set in the door leading to what was originally the Barrymore aviary. The two are portrayed embracing in a scene from *The Sea Beast*, their first film together. Barrymore was then at the height of his powers, both thespic and financial. He had recently created a triumphant Hamlet in New York and London and had just signed a multimillion-dollar contract with Warner Brothers. The world was his oyster, and he was prepared to spread its pearls at the feet of his beloved Dolores.

Described by the late Gene Fowler as "the house that Jack built," it actually is a series of seven houses, only some of which are connected by covered walkways. The main house, built above Vidor's original hacienda (which was then converted into a guest house), is approached through massive wrought-iron gates surmounted by the Barrymore crest, a crowned serpent. Seen from this distance, the towerlike structure with its white stucco walls, Italian-tiled roof, and arched patio does not appear particularly distinguished. Oddly enough, there is no place where one can stand and view the entire estate in perspective. Its true magnificence reveals itself slowly, bit by bit, as one follows the flagstone walks from garden to garden.

The first external evidence of its original opulence is the enormous circular swimming pool, completely surrounded by tall cypress, fir, and palm trees. An artificial waterfall has been cut into the fern-and-ivied slope that leads toward the house, and on the far side a great canvas-covered pavilion provides shade for resting, dining, and one can well imagine in the Barrymore days, drinking and carousing as well. The six tall wooden columns supporting the pavilion are painted in Venetian red, the awning is a terra-cotta red, and the whole effect is subtly Venetian, particularly when one glimpses the structure as reflected in the blue waters of the pool. A further memento of the past: In a patch of cement amidst the flagstones surrounding the pool are preserved the footprints of Dolores and infant John, Jr. The date is shown as 12/7/33.

As one follows the winding paths down to the other houses on the estate, the main house disappears from view completely, concealed by great stands of citrus and olive trees, cypress, and fir. The original Vidor home, built on three sides about a swimming pool, has since been graced by a tall and ancient sun and moon dial of stone, imported by Barrymore from England for a reported $15,000. Below this, and now occupied by Katharine Hepburn, who rents it from the Grimaldis, is the building that Barrymore had originally constructed for his aviary. (His collection of rare birds included a king vulture from South Africa named Maloney.) The lower floor consists primarily of a long, dark, vaulted room in which he used to entertain and show movies. A circular stairway leads up to the Tiffany door, behind which lie Miss Hepburn's Spartan quarters. She uses the vast aviary, now whitewashed and sunny, as a studio for painting.

Although little of the original furniture still remains in the graceful rooms of the main house, the Grimaldis have retained what was Barrymore's favorite possession, a beautiful Dresden chandelier that once belonged to the Emperor Franz Joseph of Austria and now hangs in their drawing room. And in a little phone room off the entrance hall is a wall that happily has never been painted: It contains scrawls, doodles, and sketches made by Barrymore himself while waiting for the Beverly Hills operators.

Perhaps the room that most closely approximates its appearance in the Barrymore days is, appropriately enough, the bar, designed to resemble a rathskeller. Paneled in polished oak and decorated with nautical scenes, the room is dominated by a vast stone fireplace surmounted by a heavy oak lintel. Oak beams support the ceiling, from which hang ship's chandeliers, and the floor is an inlay of two-foot rings of wood darkly gleaming under a high polish. The bar itself, of rich maple with blond-ash insets, Barrymore brought from a frontier saloon in Virginia City, and the huge brown cuspidor that stands beside it came from a Virginia City hotel. Hand-hewn wooden bar stools, the two antique wooden pews that flank the fireplace, and the room's heavy brown-leather furniture contribute to the sense that this is—and was—a man's world. (The heavily barred windows of this and most of the rooms on the estate suggest that Barrymore intended to keep it that way. He was known to be an intensely jealous husband.)

To the Grimaldis must go a word of special appreciation not merely for restoring, but for preserving a world and a way of life which are all but vanished today.

The Barrymore crest—a crowned serpent coiled within a crown—still adorns the gates of the vast John Barrymore estate, now owned by film-director Hugo Grimaldi and his wife. So large are the grounds that at no point can one view the entire property and its seven houses.

The bar (left), fitted like a way-side tavern, closely resembles the room when Barrymore had it. The bar itself Barrymore found in Virginia City. The floor is fitted with great rings of ancient trees, polished smooth and gleaming.

Mementos of the past: the stained-glass panel (below) depicting Barrymore with co-star—and, later, wife—Dolores Costello in The Sea Beast, *which once marked the entrance to his aviary (screen-star Katharine Hepburn lives there now); the infant feet of their firstborn, John, Jr., pressed into the cement near the pool (below, right); and adroit doodles by John, Sr., which still adorn the wall of a small telephone room just off the entrance to the main house.*

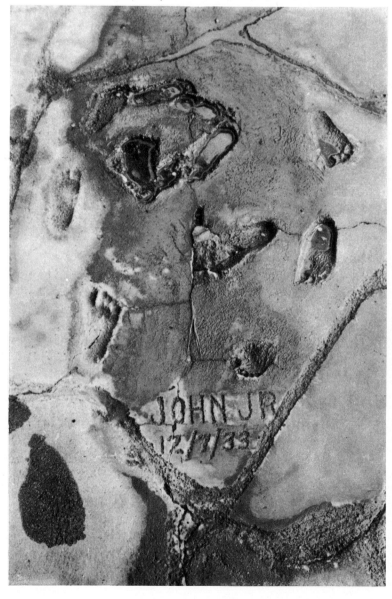

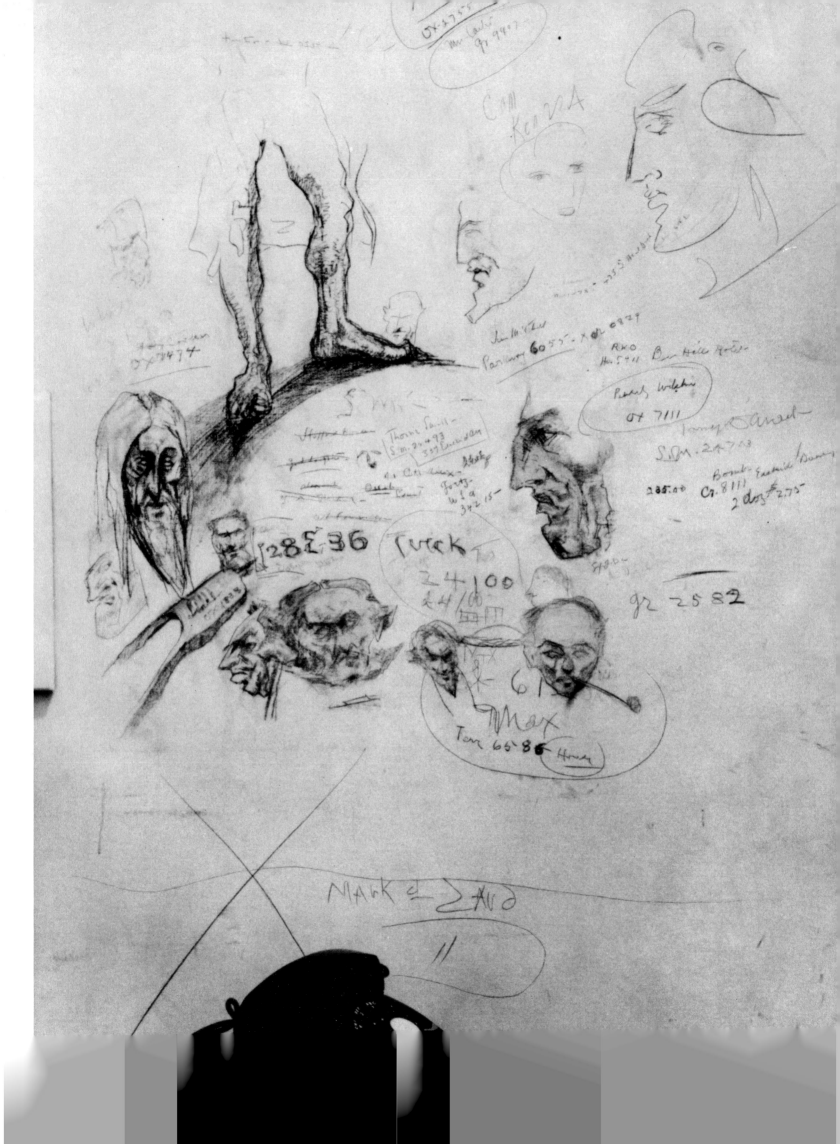

A Venetian setting—only the gondolas are missing—for a swimming pool that remains a Hollywood showplace. An artificial waterfall has been carved from the rocks on the left. The pool, with fountains playing, below.

In the years of his opulence
John Barrymore paid $15,000 to
import from England this antique
sun and moon dial. It stands
within a second swimming pool on
the estate, near the original King
Vidor hacienda.

Abby Mann
Eddie Albert

DDLY ENOUGH, though its Chamber of Commerce literature is not averse to revealing the sites of such famous Santa Monica homes as Cary Grant's, Fred MacMurray's, and Robert Mitchum's, to name but a few, no mention at all is made of the fact that Inceville, the first important studio on the West Coast, sprang up in 1912 in Santa Ynez Canyon, just north of the town of Santa Monica. Extending several thousand acres, the property was leased from the Santa Monica Water and Power Company and straddled what is now the Sunset Boulevard exit to the Pacific Coast Highway. In those days, however, the only access to the canyon was along the beach road from Santa Monica itself. Here Thomas Ince made his popular Westerns, with cowboys and Indians from the Miller Brothers 101 Ranch as the principal artists in residence. They were soon joined by Vitagraph, which opened its first western studio—a ramshackle, corrugated-iron building with a few open stages in the rear—in Santa Monica's business district.

Perhaps because of its remoteness, Santa Monica did not flourish long as a movie center. Ince soon moved to more resplendent quarters in Culver City (now the M-G-M studio), Vitagraph into Hollywood (to the site now occupied by ABC-TV). But in the opulent mid-Twenties the film colony once more discovered it—not merely for purposes of movie making but also to enjoy as residents its wide beaches, superb surf, and bracing climate. One of the first was Will Rogers, who in 1920 purchased the huge 345-acre Baca de Santa Monica Ranch north of the town; his property extended through rolling hills right down to the Pacific. "People came out to watch the beans grow," Rogers said of those early days. But as motor travel became more popular and roads, such as Sunset Boulevard, were improved, luxurious beach houses appeared along Pacific Coast Highway, most of them built by stars and executives of the movie companies who used them as weekend hide-aways.

Most opulent of all was Marion Davies', built on land purchased from the Rogers estate for $125,000. A Georgian-style white-pillared mansion, it had two swimming pools (one with fresh, one with salt water), tennis courts, and some ninety rooms, among them a vast drawing room whose ceiling was papered with fourteen-carat gold leaf, a large projection room that seated two hundred, three dining rooms, and two bars. Furnishings were resplendent leftovers from Hearst's San Simeon. Although the main house has long since disappeared, some hint of its original splendor may be gleaned from the fact that the servants' quarters now serve as the clubhouse for Santa Monica's swanky Sand & Surf Club ("Members Only").

Farther down the beach were the homes of such executives as Darryl F. Zanuck, David O. Selznick, Irving Thalberg, and Jack L. Warner; the stellar lineup included Douglas Fairbanks and Mary Pickford, Harold Lloyd, Cary Grant, and Mae West (who still has her home there). Because the beach itself is public, the properties are surrounded by fences and high walls that seal them off from prying eyes—walls, incidentally, that have proven irresistible to amateur painters. Over the years photographer Eliot Elisofon has kept a fascinating record of the ever-changing graphics and graffiti scrawled upon them. Behind these walls lie not only houses but stretches of sand, swimming pools, and often tennis courts as well.

Typical is the home formerly owned by Louis B. Mayer, for years the head of Metro-Goldwyn-Mayer and at one time the highest-salaried executive in the United States. It was acquired by Joseph P. Kennedy as a wedding present for Peter Lawford and daughter Pat, from whom it has been leased since 1967 by the distinguished screenwriter and producer, Abby Mann. President Kennedy was a frequent visitor to the house, and it is still filled with a considerable amount of Kennedy memorabilia—a bit of irony that ardent Republican Mayer would hardly be likely to relish, wherever he may be, although it accords perfectly with Mr. Mann's political tenets.

Like all the other beach houses, its back is to the mainland; a large timbered garage faces the highway, with servants' quarters above. A small open patio crowded with tropical plantings leads to the main house: five bedrooms above, a living room, dining room, kitchen, sauna, shower room, den, bar, and office below. At the far end a large pale-green living room, a few steps down, looks out toward the beach through a picture window. (All windows facing the beach are bulletproof—a memento of Mayer's labor troubles in the mid-Thirties.) The furnishings, apart from a snooker table at one end of the room, are cretonned and casual. Beyond the living room a paved patio gives access to the swimming pool and a wide strip of sand. Then comes the inevitable fence and the public beach beyond. One has the feeling in these houses that he has come upon the tycoons with their defences at least partially down. They are places more for comfort than for show. Today, incidentally, many of these homes are lived in all year round. The new freeways have put them within half an hour of any studio.

Just to the north of Santa Monica is the area known as Pacific Palisades, a model suburbia of neat tract homes, shopping centers, and a scattering of older, larger houses that went up when the Palisades was still wild and open country. This also has developed into an attractive year-round location for members of the movie colony, and particularly for those who are sports oriented. Extensive grounds permit large swimming pools and generous play areas both inside and out—as in the two-story, hacienda-style home of Eddie Albert and his actress wife, Margo, originally built in the early Thirties by silent-film star Billie Dove. A particularly pure example of the architecture that southern California has derived from Spain by way of Mexico, it is turned away from the street, its white stucco walls enclosing on three sides a large central patio that looks across miles of verdant valley to the distant Sierra Madres. The overhang of the tiled roof and timbered balconies help keep the interior cool, and fresh flowers from the gardens, plus numerous tubbed plants—such as the tree azaleas in the dining room—bring nature indoors. Because of Mrs. Albert's continuing interest in the theater, the large living room often becomes a rehearsal hall for her drama group; and because of son Edward's enthusiasm for music—he has a combo called The Lighthouse—it is frequently used for their rehearsals as well.

Particularly notable is the Albert's bar, patterned after a Mexican country *cantina*. The bar itself, under an antique kerosene lamp, is polished mahogany. Walls are white, with Cuernavaca blue stripes repeated in the blue of the ceiling, and curtains of rough white Indian cotton drape the windows. Small Mexican devil dolls—the kind exploded with firecrackers during Mexico's Fourth of July celebrations—emphasize the south of the border motif. Although the basic furnishings of the house might be found in Spanish or even French rural homes, these provide merely the backdrop for the acquisitions of a lifetime of travel: chests from Japan, chairs from Denmark and India, sculpture from Africa, books, paintings, and musical instruments from everywhere. "It's like a ship captain's home," says Mrs. Albert—but it is also charming, colorful, and eminently playable.

Overleaf:
The beach at Santa Monica, once the exclusive playground of such tycoons as Irving Thalberg,
Jesse Lasky, and Louis B. Mayer.

*The Louis B. Mayer beach house
at Santa Monica, now occupied by
writer-producer Abby Mann.
Typical of such houses, it has its
own king-size swimming pool—
and its own sand—although the
beach and the Pacific are only a
few dozen feet away. Other
devotees of year-round surf and
sun—such as Eddie Albert and
his actress wife, Margo—live in
nearby Pacific Palisades. Their
hacienda-style house (right) once
belonged to silent-film star
Billie Dove.*

Will Rogers

LARGEST OF THE private estates in the movie colony in the Twenties and early Thirties was the 345-acre ranch of the cowboy-humorist, Will Rogers, now operated (on approximately half the acreage) as the Will Rogers State Historic Park. Rogers had purchased the ranch—at the far end of Sunset Boulevard, just before it dips down to the Pacific—as early as 1920, soon after having been summoned to Hollywood to star in films for Samuel Goldwyn. At that time, however, since the comedian was more often on Broadway than before the cameras, he thought of the place as a weekend hideaway and camp-out; it did not become his permanent home until 1928, when the arrival of sound films sent his career soaring to Olympian heights. He remained there, with his wife and three children, until his untimely death in a plane crash on August 15, 1935. The property was deeded to the state for use as an historic park on August 19, 1944, after the death of Mrs. Rogers.

The house itself, now a museum, is reached by a narrow blacktop road that winds upward for several miles through a great alley of eucalyptus trees, past an immaculately tended polo field, then swings around to the parking area. The main building, yellow with a brown shingled roof, is actually three connected structures—two two-story wood-frame houses tied together by a single-storied library and sitting room. (Mr. Rogers always believed that one should not eat and sleep under the same roof.) The building on the right, with a shallow, overhanging balcony, contains the sleeping quarters and Will Rogers' study. At the south end, covered with vines, a ranch house displays most of the Will Rogers collection in one enormous two-story room. A long shaded porch leads from one house to the other.

For a man of Rogers' affluence and renown, the living arrangements are astonishingly simple and unpretentious. On the second floor the master bedroom, painted a pale beige, is quite large, but almost devoid of ornamentation of any kind apart from the hand-embroidered coverlets on its two narrow beds. Adjoining this is Rogers' office and study, a wood-paneled room with a large flagstone fireplace and a picture window overlooking his private golf course. A brass-studded leather chair stands behind his massive oaken, iron-bound desk; on it still rests the battered Remington portable on which Rogers used to compose his world-famous daily columns and the scripts of his Sunday night radio talks. Nearby stands a handsome armchair covered in red cut-velvet from which Rogers would officiate as mayor of Beverly Hills—and also nearby, the globe on which he charted the course of his ill-fated flight with Wiley Post. The only evidence that these were the quarters of a man of more than average means is a cedar-lined dressing room containing innumerable cedar closets, shelves, and drawers, and a shower stall fitted with the type of multiringed installation that one normally finds in European de luxe hotels.

Downstairs are the rooms of the children, with "Tiffanied" walls of redwood that have been hand-rubbed, painted, then rubbed again to produce a strikingly satiny effect. Again, the furnishing is sparse, with an accenting of Indian rugs, Indian scenes, and Indian dolls amidst hand-hewn wooden chairs and benches; the rooms exude a rustic charm, a feeling of having been less designed than lived in. Beyond these, leading back to the main building, is a large split-level room—paneled in knotty pine and with a handsome open-beam ceiling—that served as a combination library and sitting room. The upper level contains bookshelves and a small brown baby-grand on which daughter Mary used to perform, and the lower level comfortably groups furniture cushioned with Indian weaves about a large flag-stoned fireplace. Above the mantel a particularly fine bull's-eye mirror reflects back the entire room.

But what is (literally) the museum-piece of the Will Rogers estate is the vast ranch-style living room in the south wing. Fir-paneled and with a vast fireplace fashioned of multi-colored stone, it is roughly divided into three main areas: one for entertaining, one for dining, and a breakfast alcove in which Rogers also did much of his writing. A wicker porch-swing suspended from the rafters and covered with a colorful Indian blanket marks the division between the two main sections. The far end of the room, dominated by a shallow gallery that gives access to several small guest bedrooms above, is crammed with gifts and mementos from friends and admirers. A sarape from Tom Mix hangs at the head of the stairs (which are fashioned from polished railroad ties), and ponchos, sombreros, lassos, bolos, spurs, branding irons, and numerous fine pelts complete the collection. All of the pelts, incidentally, as well as the Texas longhorn head mounted over the fireplace, were gifts: Rogers refused to kill for sport and rarely handled firearms of any kind. He did enjoy roping, however, and in the alcove stands a small stuffed dogie that he would practice on for hours.

Highly prized are the numerous small bronzes—including one of Rogers himself— created by Western artist Charles M. Russell, a lifelong friend; and in an illuminated cabinet just below the stairway are mounted dioramas of Western views, with sculptured scenes by Russell's protégés. It also contains a valued—and valuable—pair of silver spurs, the gift of Rogers' close friend and fellow star, Leo Carillo. Together, Rogers and Carillo introduced polo into southern California; and the large picture window in the alcove—a house-present from producer Florenz Ziegfeld to his favorite *Follies* comedian—overlooks the private polo field. Now one of three such fields in southern California, the tradition of the sport is continued by the Will Rogers Polo Club, which holds matches, open free to the public, every Thursday and Saturday throughout the year.

In addition to the main house the grounds include a large garage (used primarily as offices for the museum and park), stables that can hold over sixty horses, a riding arena, several corrals, tennis courts, a golf course, and the polo field. Riding trails, laid out by Mr. Rogers himself, wind leisurely through the acres of wooded hills and open meadow. Much of this work was done during the early Thirties, when Rogers was at the pinnacle of his success and America in the depths of the Depression. To provide employment, he purposely stepped up the number of additions to his estate—and the number of men needed to work on them (over one hundred). "My own WPA," he used to call it, rejecting any suggestions of labor-saving devices that might have reduced expenses. (The stylized horses' heads supporting the ceiling beams in the main room were hand-carved by one of these workers.) In its entirety, the Will Rogers State Historic Park stands as a fitting memorial to a simple man whose acute insights and wry good humour earned him honor and affection as America's "ambassador of goodwill" to the whole world.

Cowboy-humorist Will Rogers still rides in this bronze miniature by famed Western artist Charles M. Russell.

The Rogers Museum is crowded
with relics of his long career—not
only the boots and saddles that
identified him as an authentic
cowboy but also autographed
photos of prominent Americans
(left) who regarded him as one of
our most important and influential
wits. Also preserved (right) is the
battered portable on which he
picked out his daily columns—
and the tradition of polo on his
private field (above).

Overleaf:
The main room in the Rogers
house—as simple and cluttered
as any cowpoke's bunkhouse.

81

2

Hollywood Today

THE THIRTIES dawned on a world that had suddenly, sadly changed. The crash of the stock market in 1929 put an end to an era of prosperity, free spending, and high living. What followed was the long, bitter night of the Great Depression, a period punctuated by labor unrest, by floods and dust storms in the Midwest, and by poverty and hunger everywhere. For Hollywood, the adjustment to these stringent realities of economic life was further complicated by the need to adjust to a new reality in its artistic life. Talking pictures had been in the offing since as early as 1923, when the inventor Lee De Forest began presenting his Phonofilm shorts in various theaters and auditoriums around the country. They were an interesting novelty, nothing more. Nor did enthusiasm for the new medium increase appreciably after Warner Brothers' Vitaphone made its appearance in August 1926 with a program of talking and musical shorts—including a speech by Will Hays hailing sound films as the entertainment of the future—and capped by John Barrymore, silent, as Don Juan; the feature was accompanied by a synchronized score and sound effects. What ultimately precipitated the change was the furore created by the premiere, on October 6, 1927, of Al Jolson in *The Jazz Singer*. *The Jazz Singer* was not an all-talking picture, nor had it been planned as one. The star was merely to sing three or four songs that could be readily dropped from the film for those houses not yet wired for sound; but the irrepressible Jolson turned from the piano during one of the numbers and gaily improvised some chatter with his movie "momma." It was this scene that fired everyone's imagination. Jolson was being unwittingly prophetic when he turned back to the piano with the words "You ain't heard nothin' yet!"

Although studio heads were understandably reluctant to go to the expense of reequipping their lots for what most of them were convinced was merely a passing fad, the SRO signs that appeared wherever *The Jazz Singer* was shown gave them little choice. In July 1928 *The Lights of New York*, the first all-talking picture, was released, and the panic was on. Pictures that had gone into production as silents suddenly had talking sequences written into them. Silent pictures were rereleased with synchronized scores and effects. Marquees trumpeted the first all-talking effort of one studio after another—followed by "The First 100% All-Talking Outdoor Picture," "The First 100% All-Talking 2-Reel Comedy," "The First 100% All-Talking Collegiate Comedy," and ultimately that mathematical absurdity, "The First 100% All-Talking, 100% All-Singing, 100% All-Dancing Musical." And the audiences responded in incredible numbers: Between 1927 and 1929, the first full year of sound, paid admissions were up 50,000,000 a week, jumping from 60,000,000 to 110,000,000. By 1930 silent pictures were already a thing of the past.

Because of this enormous public enthusiasm, it looked for a time as if motion pictures were going to be the nation's one Depression-free industry. Indeed, as most family budgets dwindled beyond the point where they could keep up payments on the car, much less belong to a golf or tennis club, the movies became just about the only entertainment that everybody could afford. To keep them coming, of course, the theaters had to cut admission prices drastically—often to as little as ten cents—and as the Depression deepened, to offer not only double features but also Bank Night, Dish Night, and bingo as added inducements. Purely a Depression phenomenon, the double feature has persisted as tenaciously as a bad cold.

But even though, through these expedients, attendance remained high, the studios began to succumb to the economic crisis. During the Twenties most of them had built up vast chains of theater holdings, often purchased at greatly inflated prices. As money became tight, these assets turned into liabilities, and many of the companies drifted into insolvency, then receiverships. Shoes began pinching throughout the industry; in March 1933 an across-the-board salary slash was effected in every studio, the major cuts being taken by the executives and the stars. In some cases entire staffs were dropped, then replacements hired at lower wages. Economies, often dictated by bank representatives who had little knowledge of or patience with show business, became so drastic that even the public could detect them. Some of the glamour began to rub off the word "Hollywood."

Actually, some of it had begun to disappear with the very introduction of the "talkies." Not only did sound provide a new intimacy with the actors, removing much of the godlike aloofness of silent days; it also toppled a good many from their awesome pedestals. There were stars in the large European contingent that had arrived during the Twenties, for example, who had never bothered to learn English, or who spoke it with heavy accents. Vilma Banky, Pola Negri, Greta Nissen, and Camilla Horn were among the many imported temptresses whose careers were destroyed by the microphone; for almost two years it was questioned whether Greta Garbo, M-G-M's sultry siren-in-residence, could make the transition to sound. Emil Jannings, who in 1928 won the first Academy Oscar for his performances in *The Way of All Flesh* and *The Last Command*, was on a boat headed for Germany in 1929. Even such home-grown favorites as Clara Bow, John Gilbert, and Buster Keaton had accents or voices that failed to coincide with their silent images; after a few fruitless attempts to hold their fans, all three were forced into tragic retirement. What the talkies needed were people who could handle dialogue, people with stage-trained voices. Inevitably the producers looked once more to Broadway, robbing it of some of its most prestigious stars—Fanny Brice, Ina Claire, Beatrice Lillie, Lawrence Tibbett, even the illustrious Lunts—in order to replace those whose luster had dimmed. In most instances the attempt was a failure; the audience, as ever, insisted on finding its own stars. This new galaxy included Clark Gable, Jean Harlow, Barbara Stanwyck, James Cagney, Spencer Tracy, Robert Montgomery, and such belatedly recognized old reliables as Wallace Beery and Marie Dressler. The stars may have changed, but stars remained.

Curiously, despite the incessant belt-tightening and uncertainty within the studios (and totally ignoring the economic plight of everyone outside the studios), there are many within the industry today who persist in regarding the Thirties, not the Twenties, as Hollywood's real Golden Era. Certainly, compared to what was being paid elsewhere, salaries were higher than in any other field, whether it be the $35 or so earned weekly by a "junior writer" or the $1,300,000 earned by Louis B. Mayer in 1937 (reputedly the largest take-home pay in the United States at that time). But it must also be remembered that during the Thirties the studios were turning out better than five hundred pictures a year, almost all of which were made in Hollywood. The weekly paychecks may not have been fancy by today's standards, but never again was the industry to employ so many, nor to proffer virtually continuous employment to its chosen ones. And since prices were down and taxes were low, members of the movie colony could afford to live like kings. Many of them did so.

It was in the Thirties that Beverly Hills came into its own as the new headquarters for Hollywood's stars and moguls. An independent enclave with its own government and taxes, it was laid out with wide, curving streets, shaded by graceful palms, and subdivided into lots that only the wealthy could afford. To walk the streets of

Two Hollywood landmarks: The ornate gates of Paramount Pictures and...

Beverly Hills (even today, although it's risky) is to sample the architecture of all ages and all climes. Cheek by jowl are English Tudor and Moorish minarets, pillared Colonial and French provincial, neo-Bauhaus and Frank Lloyd Wright, stately Greek temples and houses that resemble nothing so much as the pavilions of some of the smaller nations at a World's Fair. Whether in the "better" section just north of Sunset Boulevard or in the "also ran" area extending south to Santa Monica Boulevard, these large homes—all of which require at the very least an acre or two to set them off properly—nuzzle against each other with perhaps the width of a private driveway to keep them from colliding. One thing all have in common, however, is a swimming pool. To be without a private pool in Beverly Hills is every bit as *déclassé* as a Texas millionaire not having air conditioning in his Cadillac.

For all the Depression, the day of the Hollywood party had not passed—not with the likes of Lady Mendl, radio-tycoon Atwater Kent, and publisher William Randolph Hearst willing to finance the festivities, gathering unto themselves as many of the town's celebrities as their titles, prestige, and millions could command. Hearst had a great fondness for costume affairs, and lavish parties would be constructed about some preannounced theme, such as Circus Night, Venetian Night, or the Court of Louis XV Night. Hardly less formidable were the costume balls, charity bazaars, tropical *fêtes*, and garden parties arranged by the Basil Rathbones. "To commemorate their wedding anniversary," reported pundit Leo Rosten in a study of the movie colony, "the Rathbones took over the Victor Hugo restaurant, converted it into a papier-mâché cathedral and banqueted some two hundred and fifty costumed guests—with Mr. Rathbone dressed as Emperor Franz Josef and Mrs. Rathbone masquerading as Empress Elizabeth." Marion Davies thought nothing of filling her ninety-room Santa Monica beach house with an assortment of guests for a long weekend, then transforming the place into a tropical paradise by laying strips of artificial grass over the sands and importing appropriate vegetation. On only a slightly lesser plane, Errol Flynn once floated fresh lotus blossoms in his illuminated swimming pool and installed a special machine that blew multicolored bubbles for the delectation of his friends; and Sonja Henie converted her tennis court into a New York street scene, with a blue plastic sky overhead on which were projected moving clouds, for the approbation of hers. Other lavish party-givers of the Thirties included Janet Gaynor, David Selznick, and Douglas Fairbanks, Jr., then married to Joan Crawford.

As more easterners moved west, dining out in Hollywood took on a certain

The white colonnades of Warner Brothers Sunset Boulevard studio, now owned by ABC-TV.

degree of sophistication. Dave Chasen, a former vaudeville comic, had acquired such a reputation for his barbecues that in the mid-Thirties a group of his admirers staked him to a restaurant of his own—"just to get away from Musso-Frank's," Allen Rivkin, one of the original backers, recalls. Today Chasen's is one of the finest restaurants in Los Angeles. Similarly, the Lucullan dishes that came from Preston Sturges' kitchen whenever he entertained inspired the formation of The Player's Club, a restaurant whose passing is still mourned by Hollywood's more estimable gourmets. Perino's, Don the Beachcomber, Bit of Sweden, Somerset House, and several additions to the Brown Derby chain all served to broaden the culinary horizons of the town during the Thirties.

Nightclubs fared less well. While films are in production, actors and actresses may have to rise before six in the morning to make an early call—not conducive to late-night carousing. And when not involved in production, stars are far more apt to entertain at home than to offer themselves for exhibit at a tourist trap. (Even today, it is more often the starlets on the rise than the stars who have made it who turn up at such places as the Daisy and the Factory—and these are private clubs, not open to the general public.) During the Thirties the most popular spots, all of them on "The Strip" that connects Hollywood with Beverly Hills, were the Trocadero, Ciro's, and the Mocambo. None has survived, despite repeated attempts to reestablish them with new names or new policies. For the sporty crowd in the Thirties there were fight nights at Hollywood's American Legion Stadium, baseball at the Gilmore Stadium, and horse racing, now legalized, at Santa Anita and Hollywood Park. For the rich and sporty crowd there was also polo on Sundays at the fashionable Riviera Country Club, where the likes of Walt Disney, Will Rogers, and Darryl Zanuck could be found risking life and limb astride their own ponies.

During this period, it should also be noted, several of the major companies moved out of Hollywood proper, taking considerable chunks of the population along with them. Fox, which had been operating out of a small but serviceable studio at Sunset and Western, early in the Thirties began to enlarge its Westwood facility into a vast complex of stages and an enormous back lot. (When Fox sold off this back lot in the Sixties, its acreage was transformed into Century City.) Warner Brothers, despite their imposing structure at Sunset and Bronson, transferred their headquarters to a new and magnificently equipped plant in Burbank, where soon they were joined by Walt Disney's studio. Over the hill from Warner's lay Universal City; and a bit farther out in the San Fernando Valley Mack Sennett had opened a new studio for

The tourist's Hollywood: A movie premiere at Grauman's Chinese and...

the production of his Bulldog Comedies. By the mid-Thirties this had been taken over by Republic as a suitable site for its low-budget Westerns and serials. By the end of the Thirties the only major studios remaining in Hollywood proper were Columbia, Paramount, RKO-Radio, and the Goldwyn lot. As a consequence, studio people began moving out of the Hollywood hills, out of once fashionable Whitley Heights, Los Feliz, and the Rossmore district, to make their abodes in such new real-estate developments, farther west, as Brentwood, Holmby Hills, and Bel-Air; or they followed the Cahuenga Pass into Toluca Lake, Studio City, and Encino. Hollywood itself was left largely to the hot-eyed crew of hangers-on and the sun-dried band of Midwestern early settlers so harrowingly described by Nathanael West in *The Day of the Locust*. For the glamour people, Hollywood was now a place to work but no longer the place to live.

Although for twenty years Hollywood had been recognized as the movie capital of the world, during the late Thirties it became the radio center as well—a fact that had much to do with the community's rapid recuperation from the Depression years. Attracted both by the high concentration of talent and the relative cheapness and availability of land, the major networks switched so much of their programming to the West Coast that the phrase "Live—from Hollywood" became for a time part of the language. To accommodate this ever-increasing activity, CBS in 1937 opened a spacious $2,000,000 building on the corner of Sunset and Gower—the very site, oddly enough, of the Horsleys' Nestor studio in 1911. And when in 1938 NBC opened an even larger "radio city" at Sunset and Vine, its acreage included the original site of De Mille's converted barn. The process is just a bit reminiscent of the early Christian practice of erecting its churches on the ruins of former pagan temples. And can there be any significance in the fact that when these studios are torn down, their sites are invariably used for supermarkets or banks?

Just as World War I had played an important role in the creation of Hollywood, World War II contributed significantly to its transformation and decline. Not that Hollywood or its stars had lost their hold on the popular imagination. If anything, this was strengthened when, soon after New York opened its famous Stage Door Canteen, the movie colony—headed by Bette Davis, producer Sol Lesser, and talent agent Jules Stein—put together the larger and even more famous Hollywood Canteen. Probably no serviceman stationed in or passing through California between

The view from the orchestra shell of the Hollywood Bowl, since 1924 a center for music and rallies.

1942 and 1945 passed up the opportunity that the Canteen afforded to talk with the stars, dine with the stars, and dance with the stars (and always to the music of one of the "name" bands of the day). Studios, hitherto sealed tight against the general public, opened their doors to permit servicemen to see movies being made. So great was the influx, so taxed were the town's facilities, that the movie houses actually used their lobbies as dormitories where weary GIs could catch a night's sleep before once more sampling Hollywood's prodigal hospitality.

The war was also producing an influx of another kind into the Los Angeles area. With a number of Army, Marine, Navy, and Air Corps installations in the immediate vicinity, the wives and families of servicemen were arriving by the thousands. Work was plentiful and the living considerably pleasanter than what many of them had known back home—particularly with a war on. More important, many of the wartime industries—most notably aviation and electronics—had moved into the area, producing an all but insatiable demand for skilled and semiskilled workers. Since the pay was higher than in most trades or factories, they attracted still more people to the area—people who began to buy homes and settle in. Land values rose spectacularly, and San Fernando Valley, hitherto a sparsely settled farming area, was transformed almost overnight into a vast sea of small houses. Los Angeles had taken a giant stride toward becoming the megalopolis that it is today—and Hollywood had begun to lose its status as a one-industry town.

Meanwhile, the industry itself was being mobilized for war. Out in Culver City the rambling Hal Roach studio, once the home of Laurel and Hardy comedies, had been converted into "Fort Roach" for the production of Army training films— and staffed by writers, directors, actors, and technicians who only a short time before had been doing much the same sort of work, but out of uniform. Other war-related information and orientation films were being supplied by the major studios at little or no cost to the armed services, with top stars frequently contributing their services as narrators. Many others—actors like Clark Gable, James Stewart, and Robert Montgomery, directors like Frank Capra, John Ford, John Huston, and William Wyler—had left Hollywood to work in the Army Signal Corps headquarters on Long Island (in what was formerly Paramount's East Coast studio) or to go into combat. Others—Bing Crosby, Bob Hope, Martha Raye—flew under USO auspices to entertain troops in the far-flung battle zones. The contributions of the film community to the various War Bond campaigns are perhaps epitomized in the tragic death of comedienne Carole Lombard, killed in a plane crash while

Now a home for senior citizens, the Elysee was once Hollywood's most fashionable hotel.

returning from a fund-raising tour. The studios themselves, hampered by acute shortages of matériel and personnel (particularly of believably male juvenile leads), tightened their corporate belts and ground out pictures for entertainment-hungry soldiers and civilians everywhere.

For Hollywood, these were the boom years. Never before—and, as it developed, never again—did they have it so good. Every film made money, no matter what its quality. Defense plants were working on a round-the-clock basis, unemployment had virtually disappeared, and wages were rising. But in the restricted war economy, with its rationing of food and gasoline and sharp retrenchment in the production of nonessentials, there was little to spend the money on except the movies. Theaters matched the factories, staying open all night to accommodate workers headed for the swing shift or the graveyard shift in aircraft factories and shipyards. By the end of the war, according to industry estimates, attendance was up to 95,000,000 a week, not counting the GIs, who were seeing the same pictures free of charge in the various combat zones. Ticket prices were almost triple what they had been a decade earlier. As the war ended and the servicemen came trooping home, the industry's prospects looked bright. Soon, executives figured, they would have their foreign markets back as well, and profits would be greater than ever.

What these executives failed to take into account was television. A tiny black cloud on the movies' horizon when the war began, the nascent television industry was among the first to feel the effect of governmental restrictions. Experimental telecasting had already begun, yet the manufacturing of receivers was hastily abandoned when government controls clamped down on it. But no sooner did the controls come off than the production of TV sets was resumed—and TV programming as well. By 1948 enough sets were in the hands of the consumers that the studios could feel the pinch; certain nights—as when Milton Berle or the Sid Caesar–Imogene Coca *Show of Shows* were presented—were dead so far as the theaters were concerned. Such headlined events as the Kefauver crime investigations, the Army–McCarthy hearings, and each successive World Series convinced millions more that the television set had become as necessary as the telephone. And Hollywood was rapidly discovering that the day of business-as-usual was over, that ordinary pictures in the theater could not hope to compete with free entertainment in the parlor.

For the next few years it seemed there was nothing Hollywood could do that was right. Recognizing the threat of television, the studios refused to come to terms with it, permitting first the networks, then the advertising agencies to take the initiative in programming. Until the early Fifties they even refused to sell their libraries of old pictures to television, arguing that their first responsibility was to the motion-picture theaters of America; in lieu of American films, TV crowded the airwaves with cheap British movies of dubious vintage. At the same time, the studios learned that they would have to divest themselves of their precious, hard-won theater holdings by order of the Supreme Court; a suit initiated by independent theater owners shortly before the war charged that the production companies were monopolistically favoring their own chains against the interest of the independents. No action had been taken during the war years, but immediately after, in 1946, the government's "consent decrees" began coming through. Their effect could hardly have been less satisfactory for either side. Divorced from their theaters, the film

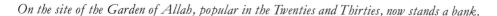

On the site of the Garden of Allah, popular in the Twenties and Thirties, now stands a bank.

One of Hollywood's best-known restaurants, the Brown Derby archly illustrates its title.

companies were no longer guaranteed an automatic outlet for their pictures and began retrenching on production. And the theater owners, faced with less product, found themselves forced to bid higher prices for whatever was offered—at a time when theater attendance was declining drastically.

As a further retrenchment, the film companies decided to eliminate their costly rosters of contract players, writers, and directors, figuring that if production was being cut back, it would be cheaper in the long run to hire them on a picture-by-picture basis than at a guaranteed annual wage. Again they were wrong. In the rapidly shrinking market, stars became of primary importance in selling a movie; and whereas a contract may have netted a top performer as much as $500,000 a year, in a very short time the studios found themselves paying them at least that much per picture—plus a percentage of the profits. For also in the meantime, personal income taxes had risen sharply while corporate taxes remained relatively low; stars, often in partnership with a writer, a director, and/or a shrewd business representative, found it expedient to incorporate. "LOOK, MA, I'M A CORPORATION" read a *Variety* headline as this practice mushroomed throughout the industry. Studio heads quickly discovered that they were no longer dealing with Burt Lancaster, Kirk Douglas, James Stewart, or Cary Grant; they were dealing with corporations of which these gentlemen were salaried employees—and the corporation was more interested in a percentage deal that promised profit participation and partial ownership of the film than in any salary, no matter how large. (Considering taxes, the well-publicized $1,000,000 salaries—always plus percentage—of Marlon Brando and Elizabeth Taylor are at least as much for prestige purposes as for income.)

That the system has worked to the stars' advantage is evidenced by many of the homes on the following pages, such as James Coburn's and Steve McQueen's. *How* it worked is intimately tied to the story of United Artists since 1950. When UA was formed in 1919, it was solely for the purpose of distributing the films of its four owners: Charlie Chaplin, Douglas Fairbanks, Mary Pickford, and D. W. Griffith. As time went by, and their volume of production was not enough to sustain the company's distribution network, other producers were invited to share the facility— Samuel Goldwyn, Joseph Schenck, Alexander Korda, Walt Disney, Walter Wanger, David O. Selznick, and others. The list was long and distinguished; within the industry United Artists was known as "the Tiffany's of motion pictures." By the late Forties, however, "Tiffany's" was becoming a bit tarnished: Its founding members had either died or become inactive; the other independents it had attracted to its banner were finding more lucrative distribution deals elsewhere. In a last, desperate effort to keep it afloat, UA was optioned to two bright New York lawyers, Arthur Krim and Robert Benjamin, who had a year to change the firm's red to black. They did so by acquiring enough product, regardless of quality, to feed its exchanges; but at the same time they put out feelers to the new independents—the stars and writers and directors who had become corporations. Given artistic freedom, would they create new films for United Artists? If the people they approached —men like Sam Spiegel, Stanley Kramer, and Burt Lancaster—would provide the "package," they would provide the money.

UA's timing was perfect. The plan that they proposed fitted precisely the new realities of film economics and the needs of the film-makers as well. In an incredibly short time Krim and Benjamin had not only removed the red ink from the firm's ledgers but had recaptured the luster that had long since vanished from the firm's

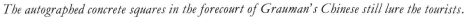

The autographed concrete squares in the forecourt of Grauman's Chinese still lure the tourists.

The Ambassador Hotel in the Thirties, when it was the scene of such Hollywood rituals as the Academy Awards.

escutcheon. A series of prestige pictures—*The African Queen, Moulin Rouge, High Noon, Marty*—demonstrated that the public could be wooed away from its television sets in satisfying numbers if provided with exceptional entertainment. They also demonstrated the superiority of the custom-made film, one created by a group of artists brought together for a specific project, to the assembly-line methods of the large film factories. Before long other studios began tentatively to try the UA approach, offering deals as good as—or better than—Krim and Benjamin's in an effort to lure top talents to their own lots. Larger percentages, greater creative control, in some instances outright ownership of the negative after a certain period of time, were the incentives being offered. By 1960, less than ten years after United Artists began their quiet revolution, the "independent deal" had become the new order in Hollywood's way of life; literally every studio had adopted it to some degree.

Meanwhile, the motion-picture industry had also worked out its *rapprochement* with television. Although in the early Fifties it continued to battle the rival medium with bigger pictures, wider screens, and 3-D, the studios succumbed one by one because of the divorce from theater operations, the shrinking box-office attendance, and the increasingly large sums that the networks were willing to pay for old pictures. Within a few years the TV screens were flooded with Hollywood's pre-1948 product—and studio executives were gleefully revealing their windfall profits to their delighted stockholders. At about the same time, in the mid-Fifties, the studios began to discover that although their own production was curtailed, their excess sound stages could be profitably rented to the numerous independent packagers who were moving into the television field with half-hour or full-hour filmed series. As the dollars poured in, it occurred to many of the studio heads that they were fully equipped to create similar packages themselves. By the dawn of the Sixties there were few studios in Hollywood that did not have their own television arm. Indeed, there are those who point out that without such television auxiliaries Hollywood might well have become a ghost town. Instead, production moved increasingly to the West Coast, centering in such vast establishments as the CBS Television City designed by William Pereira and NBC's huge installation in Burbank. The cycle was completed when MCA, a talent agency that had moved into the TV packaging business, took over the whole of Universal City and began producing both for theaters and for television. As a result, the movie colony now includes

The Ambassador's famed Cocoanut Grove, still one of the movie colony's favorite night spots.

such top TV executives as Jules Stein, Lew Wasserman, and Jennings Lang.

Today, although production continues to decline (even for television), Hollywood is anything but a ghost town. While there is little likelihood that it will ever again achieve the impressive output of the Twenties and Thirties, there is now a greater sense of economic stability in the community than perhaps at any time in its history. For one thing, most of the companies have come under the financial umbrella of such corporate giants as the Transamerica Corporation and Gulf & Western, which guarantee a continuity of production regardless of current hits or failures. For another, the studios have been reorganizing on a far more realistic basis. Gone are the padded payrolls filled with relatives, sycophants, and poker-playing cronies. Gone are the elaborate, all-expenses-paid mass press junkets to distant locations and premieres. Less frequent are the stories of $100,000 scenes that end up on the cutting-room floor, of $100,000 properties purchased and then shelved as unfilmable, or of $100,000 dressing rooms to assuage the vanity of a temperamental star. Gone, in fact, is a considerable portion of the film-making itself; every year finds more and more American pictures being shot abroad—also for economic reasons. Hollywood today is less the place where films are made than where films are made *from*. It is no coincidence that as this book was being put together, Rock Hudson was just about to leave to do a film in Dublin, James Coburn was on his way to shoot a picture in Brussels and Tangiers, and Richard Crenna was off to Italy for still another.

In line with this shrinkage of local production, the studios are also cutting back their facilities or moving to other, less expensive quarters where land values are not so high. 20th Century-Fox has long since healed the scars that followed the amputation of its back lot. Universal, which in recent years has transformed itself into a sort of real-life Disneyland, has sacrificed a portion of its own back lot to the construction of a new Hilton hotel to accommodate at least some of the thousands of visitors its tours attract each week. Metro-Goldwyn-Mayer has purchased a large tract in Conejo, far out in the San Fernando Valley, and speaks of transferring its production facilities there at the earliest possible moment. And several studios have been exploring the possibility of sharing a single lot, possibly in Malibu, to their mutual advantage and economy. Thus, the flight to the west continues; and where the studios go, the movie homes invariably follow.

No matter where these studios may go, however, as long as they remain in the

Since its opening in 1944, the graceful Bel-Air Hotel has become a center for filmland social functions.

Greater Los Angeles area (a matter of some 467 square miles), they carry with them the name of Hollywood. For Hollywood is no longer a geographical entity or, as some would have it, a state of mind: It is that golden, almost mythic place in the West where the movies come from. And perhaps that is why, after location trips that today carry them to all four corners of the globe, most American film-makers return to the homes they have made for themselves in Hollywood and its environs—Beverly Hills, Brentwood, Westwood, Bel-Air, Malibu. Hollywood may no longer be where the action is, but it remains the place where the action starts.

Edith Head

AS THE MOVIE COLONY moved west in the late Twenties and early Thirties, it was inevitable that the farms and ranches give way to the developers. Large acreages were divided, then subdivided, to provide the sites on which successful film stars and producers could erect the home of their dreams; all too often, the original buildings on the land fell to the bulldozer and the tractor. One house that mercifully escaped this fate is top costume-designer Edith Head's rambling Casa Ladera, which she and her architect husband, Wiard Ihnen, have contrived to preserve as a traditional California ranch house in the Mexican hacienda style. Constructed over fifty years ago as the main building on what was originally a sheepherding ranch, the Rancho de las Aguas, it had subsequently passed into such movie hands as Robert Armstrong, who began to give it its present form, and Bette Davis before the Ihnens acquired it some twenty years ago.

The low one-story building, constructed of whitewashed adobe, presents a rather bland façade to the visitor as he drives through the white-pillared gates and up the graveled road that leads from Coldwater Canyon to the motor court. The shallow wooden porch shaded by tropical trees also offers scant evidence of the delights that lie within, for the house itself faces inward, surrounding on three sides a vast terra-cotta–tiled patio shaded by tall trees and brightened by great tubs of flowers strategically placed about the enclosure. The fourth side looks toward the ivied slope that forms one wall of the canyon. Not only do all the rooms give directly onto this patio but, as if to accentuate its central position in the Ihnens' way of life, just off of it, under the rough-hewn timbers supporting the tiled roof, is an outdoor kitchen, an outdoor dining room, and an outdoor bar. For less clement weather, which happens occasionally in southern California, there is an indoor kitchen, an indoor dining room, and an indoor bar as well.

The interior of the Casa Ladera seems almost an extension of the patio, as if the outside were somehow brought inside. This impression arises, in part at least, from the fact that terra-cotta tiling, waxed and polished, covers many of the interior floors. while furniture of woven rattan, painted white, sustains the atmosphere of cheerful, outdoor informality. But more than that is the sunny openness of the rooms themselves. All of them, save for Miss Head's bedroom, which is French Provincial, have a pronounced Mexican flavor, with white walls setting off the burnished reds of the floor tiles. Color accents come from Mexican hats, dolls, and other memorabilia that hang in gay profusion from the walls and even from the ceiling beams, reminiscent of Mexican cantinas. Flowers seem to be everywhere. Furniture, apart from the painted rattan pieces, tends to the heavy carved woods of Spanish Colonial, often cushioned with bright Mexican weavings. The atmosphere is both informal and elegant.

A showplace of the Casa, and one of Miss Head's special favorites, is the large Mexican-style kitchen, dominated by a massive stove that seems to have been carved out of natural rock. Miss Head, as expert at cooking as she is at designing, uses only charcoal flames over a hard-wood base, which adds flavor to the food. Brick-lined and flanked by stone counters, the stove is both decorative and practical. Across from it, the serving counter, topped by terra-cotta tiles, affords generous space for food preparation; the open shelves above it display colorful glazed bowls and mugs, all surrounded by a ring of graduated earthenware pots affixed to the wall. Still more cooking utensils hang from the rafters above the stove, and hand-wrought lamps suspended from chains provide the illumination. Great standing wrought-iron candelabra contribute further to the Spanish flavor of the room. Beyond it the elegantly furnished formal dining room boasts the original floor of raw mahogany.

The grounds of Casa Ladera, which extend over five acres, include a tournament-sized tennis court, a smaller house that has been converted into an architectural workshop by Mr. Ihnen, and a former stable that now serves as a garage—although, reminiscent of earlier days, it still houses a handsome old buggy. Of somewhat later vintage, but a monument to a time when Coldwater Canyon was considered a remote outpost by most Angelinos, a gas pump stands outside the garage to give succor to stranded motorists. Life may have been slower in those days, but it could hardly have been more gracious than the present way of life at Casa Ladera.

Designer Edith Head's
authentic California hacienda is
ideally designed for outdoor living.
The deep patio under the eaves
provides space for an outdoor
dining room (left).

Overleaf:
Edith Head surrounded by
Mexican toys, sombreros, tiles,
and utensils, bringing the flavor of
the exterior indoors.

*Colorfully plumed serpents hang
from the rafters of Casa Ladera
(above, left). More utilitarian
pots and casseroles adorn the walls
of an outdoor kitchen, one of two
in the house (left and below).
A pleasant casualness, typified
by the rattan furniture and hand-
hewn table, pervades the Casa, but
it has often been the scene of some
of the movie colony's most
elegant parties.*

Alex North
Rudy Vallee

URING THE EARLY THIRTIES sound films brought an influx of fresh talent to the movie capital—actors and actresses who had first tasted fame on Broadway's legitimate stages or in that new-fangled entertainment medium, radio. These were people who had voices, people who could talk or, even better, sing. For those who decided to settle—and their number was legion—Hollywood as a place to live was already a little passé. The population trend, at least for the stars, lay westward, to Beverly Hills and beyond. In the flat stretches of the canyons off winding Sunset Boulevard palatial homes began to rise on grounds considerably larger than most of the Beverly Hills building sites. Among them, in Beverly Glen, was the hacienda-style mansion that the dynamic Al Jolson, the undisputed king of the talkies throughout the early Thirties, built for his wife and frequent co-star, Ruby Keeler. Since 1955 it has been the home of composer Alex North and his wife, Sherle.

Set well back from the road and ringed by tall eucalyptus trees, the two-story house of loose-fired brick and weeping concrete is approached through an unpaved crescent drive. Because it is built in the shape of a U, with the arms extending out to the back, it appears smaller than it really is—as is immediately confirmed when one steps into its enormous entry hall, which reaches to the full height of the house. A stairway made of railroad ties leads to the bedrooms above. Even more impressive is the living room, its walls decorated with Picasso *toro* prints and prints from Hans Erni's "Europa" series. The far end, dominated by a vast brick fireplace, is raised about a foot above the rest of the room, giving it somewhat the appearance of a stage. Above the fireplace a massive dark-brown beam serves as a mantle shelf for several Picasso ceramics as well as for two prized pre-Colombian pieces. Mullioned glass windows are set in the whitewashed brick walls flanking it. At the opposite end stands Mr. North's piano, a work table, and a grouping of furniture for listening or for conversation.

For Mrs. North, the old Jolson house with its broad white walls and high timbered ceilings of unpainted wood provided a happy solution to an irksome problem. When they moved to Los Angeles, the Norths combined the modern furnishings of their New York apartment with simple American pieces from their country place in Ridgefield, Connecticut—such as the large, weathered, deep-grained trestle table in their dining room. The Mexican interiors proved hospitable. With unifying accents of her own devising—such as the two large Moroccan rugs that Mrs. North designed for her living room and had woven in Casablanca, one in white wool with black and red circles, one in black with beige and brown circles—the styles blend into an agreeable harmony.

Beyond the living room one steps into a delightful patio formed by the three arms of the house, and looking as if it had been transplanted intact from Taxco or Cuernavaca. A giant pepper tree filters light through gracefully drooping branches, eight ancient camellia trees lend their color, and giant cacti and other tropical plants grow in profusion. In the center of this flagstoned court a large stone-well has been set in a ring of decorative mosaic; a flight of open stairs leads to the shaded balcony above and the master bedroom beyond. An altogether romantic setting, it is not at all difficult to imagine the irrepressible Jolson, a sarape over his shoulder and a large sombrero perched cockily on his head, serenading his friends here on a balmy California evening.

Although many of the stars turned westward in their search for ample acreage, others looked up into the hills above Hollywood, with Whitley Heights and the newly opened Outpost Estates as favored locations. It was here, on the very peak of a mountain, that ash-blond Ann Harding, one of the first great new stars of the talkies, and her husband, Harry Bannister, built a veritable castle in 1930. Since 1941, renamed Silvertip, it has been the proudest possession of singer-comedian Rudy Vallee. The approach to this Riviera-style estate, with its great wood balconies, stone turrets, and heavily grilled windows, is past a gatehouse and a pair of iron gates set into massive brownstone posts, then up a private road to a motor court where a power-driven turntable swings the cars about and points them down the hill again.

From the entrance hall a circular staircase with red tile steps leads up to a handsome rotunda, and this in turn opens upon a beautiful sunken living room. Spanish in flavor, it is dominated by a huge rock fireplace, fourteen feet wide and ten feet high, framed by dark timbers that rise up to support the massive ceiling beams. The furniture—heavily carved Spanish chairs and sideboard, print-covered couches angled toward the fireplace—is appropriately scaled to the room's proportions. On the far wall, centered above the sideboard, hangs an excellent likeness of the attractive Mrs. Vallee.

Silvertip is filled with delightful surprises: a secret staircase that winds about the rotunda up to a sun deck, a handsome dining room furnished with authentic Italian antiques, a vast cross-timbered hall with paneled walls which serves as a music room, a covered patio carved out of natural rock which commands a view of much of the San Fernando Valley. But the real surprise is a separate four-story "fun house" built into the slope below the main house. Its flat roof, standing a few feet above the courtyard, provides a championship-sized tennis court; a flagstoned walk leads to the entrance below, marked by a blue-and-white–enameled street sign— "Rue de Vallée"—picked up in Paris. Beyond it lies a long red corridor lined on either side with shallow, semicircular arches—eighteen in all, each with its own overhead light—in which hang memorabilia marking the high points of a career that has spanned more than three decades.

A large theater (complete with projection equipment) lies to the right of the corridor, capable of seating some 125 guests comfortably, and with a fully equipped stage at the far end. Beyond this, in knotty pine, is a large playroom and bar, with a rock fireplace as large as the one in the main house. The playroom leads into what Mr. Vallee calls his Christmas Room—a long glass-enclosed porch fitted with gold-framed redwood panels in which are displayed the Christmas cards received across the years from his innumerable friends in show business. The floors below the playroom and theater are used for storage purposes—but what they store, in addition to an extensive and choice wine cellar, is a priceless collection of Mr. Vallee's recordings, orchestrations, and musical instruments, plus the saxophones of Rudy Wiedoeft and Benny Krueger, two men who played an important part in his career.

In his autobiographical *My Time Is Your Time* Rudy Vallee noted, "The remarkable place I happened upon and bought in Hollywood I wouldn't trade today for the Taj Mahal." One visit is enough to understand why.

Also in the California-hacienda style, with Mexican accents, is the home of composer Alex North and his wife, Sherle. Broad open spaces, emphasized by specially woven rugs designed by Mrs. North, mark the large living room (above). The patio (right) could almost be a set for a movie.

Spanish tile, Mexican bibelots,
and early-American furniture
blend harmoniously against the
white walls and ceiling beams of
the Norths' dining room (below,
A). At the far end of the living
room (below, B) a spacious
area doubles as Mr. North's
studio and a conversation center.

A

B

A

B

The Mediterranean-style house
of singer-comedian Rudy Vallee,
showing unique car turntable
(above, A). The large living room
(left), with its massive beams,
is dominated by a rock fireplace
fourteen feet wide and ten feet high
and an attractive portrait of
Mrs. Vallee. To the right of the
main house, extending four stories
below a champion-style tennis
court, is a combination play and
storage area. The blue and white
"Rue de Vallee" mat (above, B) marks
the entrance.

The main hall in Rudy Vallee's "fun house" is a long red corridor filled with the memorabilia of his career (left, above); in the floors below are stored orchestrations, recordings, sheet music, musical instruments—and theater posters—ever ready to be pressed back into service (left, below).

West of the rotunda shown above, Rudy Vallee's enormous music room. Like most of Silvertop, the huge windows command a superb view of San Fernando Valley.

George Cukor
Jean Negulesco

OR MORE THAN three decades George Cukor and Jean Negulesco have been widely regarded as two of Hollywood's most tasteful directors, and their homes, although totally disparate, reflect that quality. Mr. Cukor acquired his in 1930, soon after his arrival in the movie colony. Theater-trained, he had been brought to the studios originally as a dialogue director, but within a year he had become a full-fledged director and decided to cast his lot with the new-fangled "talkies." The home he bought, in the hills just east of Beverly, was then little more than a cottage. Over the years he enlarged it, however, and with William Haines as his interior decorator, furnished it with exquisitely chosen and skillfully combined period pieces. The gardens, a later addition, extend to the south of the house and are the work of Florence Yoch. Literally carved out of the hill that surrounds the property, they provide delightful shaded walks that wind upward past pergolas, small pools, and pieces of Italian sculpture acquired from an English collection. Rare and beautiful trees were moved in, and a wall and thick plantings were added to insure complete privacy. To Mr. Cukor's intense satisfaction, the effect is now so natural, so uncontrived, that one has the sensation of walking through the park of an ancient Italian villa rather than a Beverly Hills garden.

The house itself, which stands on a white-bricked terrace above a flagstoned court, is essentially a rambling, one-story frame structure (although a guest room, carved out of the hill at the far end, creates a second level). Painted white, its exterior seems composed almost entirely of floor-to-ceiling windows, punctuated by slender supporting columns. This feeling of sunny openness characterizes every important room in the house, particularly the formal drawing room, with its great bayed window, and the less formal—but no less elegant—sitting room that Mr. Cukor characterizes as the Oval Room. Grouped under the superb Waterford crystal chandelier in the drawing room are a set of three French Regency armchairs from the early eighteenth century, their seats and backs covered in tapestries illustrating fables from La Fontaine; a fourth armchair is eighteenth-century Austrian, covered in needlepoint upholstery; all four face an eighteenth-century English settee that all but fills the bay. On either side of the window stands an elaborate English Regency commode with black lacquer finish, topped by large, sumptuously carved, antique Chinese Chippendale mirrors. Another conversational grouping at the opposite end of the room includes a pair of Hepplewhite barrel-type chairs covered in white leather and a Louis XV–style antique Hepplewhite sofa. Paintings include a Renoir pastel and a Grant Wood oil.

Most striking and original is the Oval Room, its broad, curving walls covered in a soft tan suede topped by a copper cornice that conceals the room's indirect lighting. Although frequently used for business conferences as well as for entertaining, the room is essentially a picture gallery, with each work beautifully displayed. Above the brick fireplace, flanked by ancient Tibetan horns of copper and brass, hangs a superb Braque still life. Other paintings are by John Ferran, Juan Gris, Georges Rouault, and Graham Sutherland; the sculpture pieces include a lovely bronze by Rodin, a Greek Venus, and an Egyptian head dated c. 700 B.C. (the latter two from the Hearst collection). Beyond this, a narrow, picture-lined passageway, filled with framed photos of Mr. Cukor's famous friends and admirers, leads back to his office and library. "A home is an accumulation of one's life," he once observed, and nowhere is this more evident than in the shelves of autographed first editions of such writers—and friends—as Noel Coward, Aldous Huxley, Thomas Mann, Somerset Maugham, and the Sitwells, the striking charcoal-and-pencil drawing of a youthful Ethel Barrymore by John Singer Sargent, or Cecil Beaton's stunning sketch of Katharine Hepburn. In formal informality George Cukor lives surrounded by the things he loves and by the mementos of those who loved him.

In striking contrast is the Beverly Hills home of director Jean Negulesco, whose previous tenant had been the glamorous Greta Garbo. Where Mr. Cukor's house is redolent of eighteenth- and nineteenth-century gentility, Mr. Negulesco's is ablaze with a first-rate sampling of the challenging art of this century. Himself an artist of distinction, Jean Negulesco was among the first to champion the paintings of Bernard Buffet in this country, subsidizing his work during the dark years before recognition arrived. In consequence, the vast Negulesco rear living room (the house has two living rooms) contains perhaps the largest privately owned collection of Buffets in the world. Other modern masters represented in the extensive collection are Modigliani, Rouault, Toulouse-Lautrec, and Henry Moore. But impressive in their own right are the bold, swirling line drawings that flank the circular stairway leading to the bedrooms above—and these are the work of Jean Negulesco himself.

"The Seasons," Italian sculpture from an English collection, graces the extensive gardens of George Cukor's secluded Beverly Hills estate.

The Cukor home, filled with the framed portraits, autographed books, and paintings of his many close friends, has been furnished by designer William Haines with a choice selection of eighteenth- and early nineteenth-century antiques. Typical is the drawing room (below), with its French Regency chairs, English Regency commodes, and Chinese Chippendale mirrors.

Overleaf:
Handsome in its simplicity is Mr. Cukor's Oval Room, finished in tan suede topped by a copper cornice.

Director Jean Negulesco, a prize-winning painter before turning to the movies, drew the swirling line drawings that fill the stairwell of his Beverly Hills home. A noted patron of the arts, he owns an outstanding collection of modern and contemporary paintings—including the largest private collection of Bernard Buffets in this country.

The Green Bedroom of the
Negulesco house formerly contained over a dozen Rouaults.
When guests complained they
interfered with sleep, the number
was reduced.

The dining room is furnished
in dark, rich woods that set
off authentic Picasso plaques
in the handsome breakfront.

Ira Gershwin
Natalie Wood

URING THE THIRTIES, after the movies had learned to talk, composers and song writers suddenly discovered that for them, too, Hollywood had become a Promised Land. Not only was there a vogue for musicals, but serious dramas, producers were quick to learn, gained substantially in their effectiveness with the addition of an evocative score. Notable among the recruits from New York's musical-comedy stage were George Gershwin and his talented lyricist brother, Ira, and another gifted lyricist, a close friend of the Gershwins, E. Y. "Yip" Harburg. For the past half-dozen years or so, the Harburg house, where *Finian's Rainbow* was written, has been the home of actress Natalie Wood.

Although the Gershwins had been making periodic sorties into movieland since as early as 1930, they did not decide to make the arrangement permanent until 1936, at which point the two brothers leased a large Spanish-style house in Beverly Hills. It was next door to the one that, completely remodeled along neo-Regency lines, is now the home of Ira and his charming wife, Leonore. This house, set well back from the street to permit a curving driveway to the door, has a rather small, elegantly marbled entryway that gives immediately onto a large, and even more elegant, formal drawing room. At the far end, against a wall of bleached wood, stands George Gershwin's grand piano, flanked by a magnificent Modigliani and a Picasso. Indeed, the entire home is a miniature museum of modern art, with prints and oils by many of the great twentieth-century painters, plus a scattering of sculpture and statuary. Since both Gershwins, Ira and George, had always been avid, and gifted, painters and sketchers, many of their works are also represented in the collection—although, with characteristic modesty, Ira hangs these in the less frequented rooms of his house.

Beyond the drawing room, with its bleached-wood floors and champagne-colored furnishings, lies a less formal sitting room that overlooks a lush garden and tennis court. Light flows in from a canopied patio through floor-to-ceiling windows, bouncing off the light woods of the walls and accentuating the whiteness of the furniture and its bright yellow cushions. Copper-pipe radiant heating circulates beneath its white terrazzo floor. To the right of this room is the Gershwins' marvelous kitchen, with twin stoves and chopping blocks centered among neatly concealed pantry shelves, wall ovens, and refrigerators. To the left a stylized bronze horse from India stands guard at the foot of a gracefully curving, sunlit stairway that leads to the bedrooms above. And beyond the stairway, down a short picture-lined passage, lies a game room with a champion-sized billiard table. At one end stands a famed Siqueiros painting of George Gershwin performing in concert (which the Gershwins have now donated to the University of Texas); at the other end, its desk overlooking the gardens, is Ira Gershwin's workroom. Because it freely mingles the art and the furniture of many periods and many lands, the

Gershwin house conveys a sense of elegant informality, of patrician taste keyed to comfortable living.

Natalie Wood's lovely home is far less formal, but no less tastefully arranged in its informality. Its exuberantly planted garden, shaded by a large, spreading holly tree, includes innumerable hideaway nooks, an impressive exercise area, and a large, irregularly shaped pool flanked by tan rocks overhung with vivid bougainvillea. Twin arborvitae in tubs mark the entrance to the living room, with its unobtrusive gray textured walls and carpeting. At one end a large single timber forms the mantle shelf over a fireplace decorated by dark, polished woods encrusted with onyx. A curving, cushioned settee fills the bay window looking out over the garden; it is the focal point for one of several conversational groupings of furniture in the room. At the far end stands a green piano surmounted by an excellent Courbet, and on either side of a small bar hang two large abstracts by Gerald Silva, a young California artist. At the foot of the stairway leading up to the working and living quarters above, which is completely lined with watercolors and prints, Miss Wood has placed a large, glowing Bonnard. Beyond it lies a den, which houses the major portion of her extensive collection of pre-Colombian art.

Since the house, designed in the early Thirties by Negro architect Paul Williams, is constructed on the downslope of a hill, its main entrance, quite small, is actually on the second story. Just to the left of it is Miss Wood's office, finished in a gray wood, its walls crammed with pictures, plaques, and awards; opposite the windows a shelf bears the larger trophies. A cushioned, built-in couch covered in black and white cretonne, three comfortable director's chairs, and a workmanlike desk complete the room. The same gray carpeting that is downstairs runs throughout the house.

To the right of the entry lies the master bedroom, dominated by a queen-sized bed over which hangs a white lacy canopy. The bedspread is of tufted pink-and-green–flowered cretonne, and the headboard is of Mexican design, painted an off-white. Cretonne curtains matching the spread hang at the bay window, which has a pink-cushioned sofa built into it. Crystal chandeliers suspended from brass chains are on either side of the bed, and next to it a low French breakfront provides a night table. A gold and glass vanity, a few tiny chairs of blue wicker, and great glassed-in clothes closets give the room a lightness and femininity that is wholly delightful.

Beyond it, at the far end of the house, lies Natalie Wood's sitting room, perhaps the most formal room in the house. Finished in blue and beige, it has as its centerpiece an elegant blue and gray French breakfront with gilt trim, containing a number of Wedgwood plates, cups, and bowls. More Wedgwood pieces grace a fragile table of glass and gold. Two large blue sofas and white wicker furniture with powder-blue cushions sustain the Wedgwood motif, as do the room's five closets with blue floral prints on each door. It is an intimate, comfortable, handsome room, and quite rightfully, Miss Wood takes considerable pride in the fact that she designed it—and all the rooms in her house—herself.

A 200-pound bronze horse from India stands guard at the foot of the Gershwin staircase. Lacy grillwork and glass flood the house with sunlight.

*Ira Gershwin and friend (above).
White terrazzo floors, indoor
plants, and pale pastel fabrics
provide a cheerful yet neutral
background for one of the outstanding private collections
of modern painting and sculpture
in the United States.*

*Overleaf:
The Gershwins' sitting room.
Floor-to-ceiling windows
look out toward a canopied patio.
Note Modigliani over mantel
shelf and extensive art library.*

Ira Gershwin stands in his Beverly Hills drawing room (left) by brother George's grand piano, flanked by Modigliani and Picasso paintings. He shoots pool (below) with actor Richard Conte before a famed Siqueiros painting of George Gershwin performing in concert; this game room is also his office and workroom.

Actress Natalie Wood in a poolside workout (right). Her home formerly belonged to lyricist E.Y. Harburg.

Surrounded by the photos, trophies, and awards of a career that began when she was four, Natalie Wood studies a new script in the office of her Beverly Hills home (above) and chats with author Arthur Knight in her living room (right). Miss Wood takes pride in the fact that she did all the decorating herself.

The Wood house, built in the early
Thirties, was designed by architect
Paul Williams, whose "Father
Winter" is prominently dis-
played in its garden (below).

133

Despite the Mexican headboard, the dominant tone of Natalie Wood's bedroom is delicately, elegantly feminine and French.

Gypsy Rose Lee

HERE COMES A TIME in one's life," says actress-writer-painter and one-time ecdysiast Gypsy Rose Lee, "when you want to wake up in the morning surrounded by familiar things—the same house, the same furniture, and if you're lucky, the same man." It was this attitude that prompted Miss Lee, when she moved to California in 1961, to bring with her the furnishings and decorations of her New York home and re-install them in the seventeen-room Beverly Hills mansion she bought at that time. The result is one of the most personal and exciting homes in the entire movie colony—gay, colorful, unique.

The house itself, Italian Mediterranean in style, was built in the early Twenties atop one of the highest of the Beverly Hills and covers some two acres. Miss Lee had to install a high retaining wall, which she reports "is built like Hoover Dam," and fronted it with tall cypresses that add to the Mediterranean effect. Between the wall and the house is a small swimming pool—"really, just a plunge," she says—and a well-tended garden, complete with a shallow moat stocked with goldfish (named after some of her more famous friends) which extends around one end of it.

But the real delights are on the inside, whose exuberant decor defies labels of period or place. The drawing room, for example, is almost like a stage setting, with a flight of polished steps leading down into it through a graceful archway overhung by a curving, golden organ-loft. (There is no organ, but a 16mm projector is occasionally stationed here for film shows.) The far end, three steps below the room itself, is a marvelous atrium composed of five arched windows and a glass-domed roof; at the turn of the tap it can be deluged by tropical rains that drain into the moat just beyond it. Luxuriant tropical plantings fill the atrium, and their greenery is reflected in the rich draperies created by Robin Huntington and in the green satin cushions of the Regency chairs and chaise longue. Small tables—including one topped in leather on which are painted scenes of Wellington's victories—provide intimate conversational groupings, and the room's sense of theater is augmented by a vaulted, gold-painted ceiling and gold walls that create a glowing background not only for the furnishings but also for the innumerable works of modern art that adorn her walls. Over the mantel a large portrait of Miss Lee by Rudi Bernatschke depicts her in that very room.

Dark greens, gold, and brown dominate the drawing room; by contrast, the dining room, with its pale-blue walls and silver and gold cloud-painted ceiling, its gay crystal chandelier and vast picture window, is light, gay, and informal—"almost like eating outdoors indoors," Miss Lee likes to say. Its huge green table, with matching lazy Susan, can seat twelve intimately (if not altogether comfortably) on large, curlicued wrought-iron and wicker chairs, also painted to match. (The table, incidentally, stands on the wrought-iron legs of old Singer sewing machines that she painstakingly collected over the years.) It is a room for the enjoyment of food—quite properly, since cooking is another of Gypsy Rose Lee's great passions and talents. For confirmation of this enthusiasm, one need only step into her kitchen. Skillets, casseroles, saucepans, and pots of all shapes and sizes hang in giddy profusion from a mobile designed by her ex-husband, painter Julio de Diego, who also made the embossed copper ventilator shield over the stove and the metal shades for the lights. There are open shelves for cookbooks, open shelves for glassware and crockery, open shelves for spices and, also on these shelves, wood and glass bins from Denmark for grains and condiments. A painting by Gromaire hangs over the electric range.

The second floor, reached by a curving staircase lined with etchings and watercolors by such artists as Dufy, Tchelitchew, Vertès, and de Diego, consists of two bedrooms with connecting bath. The guest room, decorated in tones of mauve and green, uses curtains at the many windows and behind the bedstead to graceful yet dramatic effect. (The color coordination, incidentally—here and throughout the house—is the work of designer Jane Ashley.) The wood and iron bedstead—quite narrow, but beautifully carved and painted—stands between two arched, curtained windows and has an arched curtain of its own, somewhat higher, hanging behind the headboard. Overstuffed chairs and sofa embroidered in floral patterns, a mirrored umbrella-and-hat stand, and a dark shaft bearing artificial flowers under a crystal dome contribute echoes of Victorian elegance which add considerably to the room's piquance. As in Miss Lee's own bedroom, the ceiling is decorated with floral wallpapers that Miss Lee scalloped with her own hands.

Perhaps the most extraordinary room in the house, however, is Miss Lee's malachite-green bathroom, with rich purple accents. Hede Fischer, an artist friend, came in from New York to hand-paint the designs on the exterior of the tub as well as the flowers painted behind the glass of the curtained mirror that dominates one wall of the room. She also decorated the intricately carved wood and wicker frame, obtained from the Swedish Embassy, that chastely conceals the commode. The large painted-wood washstand also projects the feeling of an earlier, more elegant time.

"A home is the things that are in it, the things that you know and love," says Miss Lee. And every room is loaded with the toys, treasures, and souvenirs—"dusty things," she calls them—that reflect the taste, individuality, and flair that have earned her success as a writer, artist, actress, and in recent years as an outstanding television personality and hostess.

Gypsy Rose Lee's bedroom (above) and guest room (above, right). Miss Lee cut by hand from wallpaper the floral patterns that brighten the ceilings of these colorful rooms.

Two views of the connecting bath.
The commode (below, left) is
attractively concealed, and the
ornamented tub (below, right) is
reflected in a curtained, hand-
painted mirror.

Gypsy Rose Lee's drawing room
(above and right) provides a
glamorous, theaterlike setting for
art and artifacts collected during
her long and multifaceted career.

A noted hostess and chef,
Miss Lee loves to entertain in the
graceful, sunny dining room
(below), serving gourmet dinners
that she creates in her well-stocked
kitchen.

Francis Lederer

IN 1933 Francis Lederer, already an international star of films and theater, began to build his showplace home in Canoga Park, a distant suburb of Los Angeles which in those pre-freeway days was almost a full day's journey from the center of the city and a good four hours from the heart of Hollywood. Czech-born and newly arrived in the movie capital, Mr. Lederer had fallen in love with the California-mission style of architecture, which seems to combine the best of both possible worlds—the Italian classicism of the Renaissance and the eclecticism of the early Spanish colonials, who contrived to fuse the arts of their native land with the native materials of southern California. This fusion of past cultures—Italian, Spanish, and Californian—characterizes every square foot of the Lederers' fascinating Canoga Mission Park.

The approach to the house is through a private road lined with pepper trees, lighted by night with great *flambeaux*, winding up to a vast plateau overlooking much of the San Fernando Valley. The house itself, still under construction after more than three decades, extends in a U-shape about a large court of rough, multi-colored brick. In one corner of the court a round, weathered table and comfortable red-cushioned chairs are grouped close to an open, wood-burning fireplace surmounted by a semicircular della Robbia plaque. All about the stone and brick patio, with its low, overhanging tiled roof, other plaques and antique fragments decorate the walls, illuminated by small iron candleholders. Immediately, one is transported back through the centuries, but back more to a sense of old, evangelical *padres* than of fierce, exploitative *conquistadores*. The Lederers' Mission Park is like a shrine devoted to religion and to art, not to a flamboyant display of the fruits of conquest.

This feeling is admirably sustained throughout the interior—in the spacious, somewhat austere rooms with their white, rough-bricked walls, timbered ceilings, and heavy accent of ancient religious paintings and sculpture, and particularly in the monastic archways and corridors that lead from room to room. Religious art and artifacts are everywhere: paintings, sculpture, plaques, mullioned stained-glass windows, church candelabra, and the ornate, heavy crucifixes of the Renaissance. Veronese, Pisano, Bandinelli, and Alonso Cano are among the artists represented in the Lederer collection, and a number of fifteenth-century della Robbia pieces dominate the sculpture. Massive, richly carved credenzas, chests, and catafalques; antique, intricately paneled doors; and outsized tables and chairs of various polished woods contribute to a sense of the living past, a sense further accentuated by the red terra-cotta floors with their inlays of the Lederers' own specially designed blue-and-white–tile medallions.

Literally the center of the house, for everything else flows out from it, is the vast thousand-square-foot living room furnished—except for its comfortably modern sofa facing toward the open fireplace—with fifteenth-century pieces, primarily of Florentine origin. A richly painted statue of the Madonna, flanked by exuberantly carved columns and recessed in a tapestry-lined niche, dominates one end of the room, accompanied by two smaller saint figures set in niches of whitewashed brick on either side. Balancing these at the other end is a massive Italian credenza, also flanked by columns, bearing a mirrored, carved altar that reflects a thirteenth-century Roman crucifix and four stately bronze candelabra. Among the art treasures in this room is the Lederers' Veronese.

To the right of the living room, through a series of arches, one catches a glimpse of one of the two della Robbia figures that are perched on either end of Canoga Mission Park's unique bar. The counter, solidly built of white brick topped by terra-cotta, is about twenty feet long, recessed on the far side for the storage of glasses, bottles, and a sink; beyond it, dominating the entire wall, is an oval painting of Christ ascendant. Three walls of this irregularly shaped room are wainscoted in wood paneling that forms the back of a vast deep couch, also of white brick, fitted with three quilted terra-cotta–colored cushions. A white brick table, set at an angle to the bar and formed like an inverse pyramid, is inlaid with terra-cotta tiles and the small blue and white Lederer plaques.

No less unique—and no less beautiful for all its utility—is the Lederers' kitchen, with its modern electric stove imbedded in a great terra-cotta counter. Open shelves on either end display a multicolored array of spices, condiments, canned goods, and breakfast foods; centered in the wall above the range is yet another della Robbia, a serene Madonna surrounded by a garland of fruit. Beautifully carved wooden panels set in white plaster not only conceal the pots and pans but also carry the sense of the past into this, the most modern room in Canoga Mission Park. To the left of the counter two terra-cotta–colored electric ovens have been built into the wall, surmounted by recessed shelves holding colorfully glazed earthenware casseroles. To the right, beyond the massive oak door leading to the butler's pantry, hanging shelves display a portion of the Lederers' priceless collection of pre-Colombian art.

Below the house itself, just off the main road that runs through Canoga Park, is the stable, also built by the Lederers, despite the fact that it looks at least three hundred years old. Constructed entirely of stone quarried on the ranch and topped by a roof of Spanish tile, it houses the Canoga Mission Community Art Center, which under the direction of Mrs. Lederer is devoted to the exhibition of works by contemporary artists. But if the stable provides a delightful gallery for modern art, the whole of Canoga Mission Park can be considered as one vast museum, an exquisite setting for the arts of other periods and other places. Fittingly, Mr. Lederer, for years the mayor of Canoga Park, has already donated his house and its surrounding lands to Los Angeles County for eventual use as a public museum and park.

The entrance patio of Canoga Mission Park (left). Built by actor Francis Lederer in authentic California-mission style, the house is decorated with religious art from the fourteenth fifteenth, and sixteenth centuries —such as the life-size sixteenth-century Spanish saint (below) standing in a niche at the far end of the living room.

Two kneeling della Robbia figures grace the white brick bar of Francis Lederer's Canoga Mission Park (far left), and a fruited della Robbia wreath hangs over the terra-cotta–tiled kitchen range.

Overleaf:
The vast living room at Canoga Mission Park, with a view of the bar through central arch.

*The Lederers' dining room
(left), reminiscent of a monastic
refectory, sustains the Spanish
flavor through antique chairs and
church candelabra; heavy woods,
carvings, and tiled floors extend the same note into the library.*

Kirk Douglas, Henry Fonda, Rupert Allan, Frank McCarthy

ANY OF HOLLYWOOD'S (or, to be more accurate, Beverly Hills') most attractively modern homes are skilled remodelings of the Spanish-style architecture that had been popular thirty or forty years earlier. While the thick stucco walls and shaded patios of such houses afforded ample protection against the California heat, they also managed to eliminate much of California's vaunted sunshine. Remodeling, therefore, tends to be in terms of stripping away walls and replacing them with great glass picture windows, lending a decidedly modern, functional feeling to the houses, with air-conditioning installed to combat the temperatures. And opaque plastics have made it possible to open up other wall areas to the sun without sacrificing any of the privacy that the famed inhabitants require.

A superior example of this type of reconstruction is the Kirk Douglas home, acquired in 1956. As originally built by an oil tycoon, it was, in Mrs. Douglas's description, "a square box." The "box" has been altered considerably by the extension of a one-story carport on the north end of the two-story house, flanking a semicircular driveway and parking area. (What had been the garage, a separate building to the rear of the main house, is now a marvelous combination of projection room and game room, complete with its own piano, TV, Ping-Pong table and jukebox, its walnut paneled walls laden with trophies from Kirk Douglas's numerous hunting and fishing expeditions.)

But the main transformations are visible only on the inside. Doorways have been raised to the maximum heights permitted by the basic architecture, and small windows replaced by large sliding glass doors. Sun floods the white, beige and yellow living room through a specially constructed set-back roofed by corrugated blue plastic. The bar, of curved travertine topped by heavy mahogany, looks out toward the pool and the tennis courts beyond through floor-to-ceiling windows where once had been stucco walls. Beyond a rather narrow formal dining room, light pours into a graceful and colorful *lanai* through plastic strips set high in the white walls.

A favorite room of the Douglases is the snug den, just to the right of the bar area. Again, one wall is glass, looking out to the pool and the gardens. Opposite the entry, however, the black stone fireplace is surrounded by an impressive expanse of gray travertine, which seems to have been the cue for the striped gray and white upholstery of the easy chairs. African sculpture fills the shelves beyond, while on the adjacent wall racks of books and magazines are topped by a shelf of pre-Colombian pieces. Paintings by Barnabé, Lorjoue and Miró, and a large Picasso vase, complete the room.

Most of the family living at the Douglases takes place upstairs, reached by a stairwell lined with Clavé sketches of settings and costumes for Roland Petit's ballet version of *Carmen*. Here their two sons, Eric and Peter, each has a room—"furnished with just a bed and a rug," their mother says—which the boys have fitted out entirely to their own tastes. Adjacent to these is the master bedroom and a combination study and den, unified by a wall-to-wall green shag rug and including a small bar and stove. Off of this is Kirk Douglas's dressing room, its three closet walls fitted with sliding doors of blond wood. It is Mr. Douglas's pride and Mrs. Douglas's despair: Dominating it is an exercise machine with weights, pulls and a chinning bar that almost fills the room and must be skirted carefully to reach the washbasin on the far wall. But like everything else in the Douglas house, it is both functional and attractive.

Similarly, Henry Fonda's home in fashionable Bel-Air, just west of Beverly Hills, is also a modern remodeling of a highly traditional house. Built in 1928 in a Spanish-cum-Mexican style, it surrounds a delightfully planted patio, while the main entry is from a large, circular motor court with a garage to the right and workrooms to the left. The exterior is white (even the tiled roof has been painted white) with a black trim. Yet another patio, to the east of the house, provides a large area for dining and entertaining, from which a double flight of tan flagstoned steps leads down to the pool and the almost two acres of garden beyond.

The interior retains its Mexican aura largely through the lavish use of varishaped dark red tiles on the floors of the corridors and many of the rooms. As selected by designer Peter Shore, however, the furnishings tend to blend together French, Italian and Spanish provincial, with most of the rugs specially woven in Portugal; but the paneled doors are authentically Mexican—and removing from them the black paint applied by a previous owner is one of Mr. Fonda's prouder achievements.

Again, considerable remodeling has gone into the house itself. What was once a porch that opened onto the inside patio has now been glassed in and transformed into a graceful *galleria* which, because of its luxuriant plantings, still seems at least

*"Our own Grauman's Chinese,"
the Kirk Douglases describe
these autographed squares of
cement leading to their projection
room.*

partially outdoors. Similarly, the master bedroom on the second floor of the main part of the house was enlarged by enclosing the terraces opening off of it. A picture window installed at the far end of the living room, overlooking the pool, and floor-to-ceiling sliding glass doors in the adjacent library and den add to the sense of modernity happily wedded to tradition.

A more recent example of this wedding of the modern and the traditional is the Beverly Hills home shared by film publicist Rupert Allan and producer (formerly Brigadier General) Frank McCarthy. Built in 1956 on what had once been King Vidor's tennis court and later John Barrymore's bowling green, it is actually two houses connected by a patio and by a covered gallery lined with art posters and sculpture pieces. The two men share the patio, the pool beyond it, and an art-filled living room that commands a breath-taking view of most of Los Angeles.

Designed by art director Lyle Wheeler to afford both men the maximum privacy, the white stucco and redwood houses combine elements of the traditional Spanish with sliding doors, screens and panels reminiscent of the Japanese. Chinese temple dogs flank the entrance, fashioned from antique Louis XIV cupboard doors. The immediate vista, across the bricked patio, is of the pool, the pool terrace and, be-yond these, a steep bank planted in azaleas, cypress and ivy. To the left is Rupert Allan's suite, crammed with books and art objects, most of them collected abroad. To the right is the two-story home of General McCarthy, with his bedroom and study on the first floor and the second floor given over almost entirely to the com-munal living room, its walls lined with their distinguished collection of prints, lithographs and watercolors. It is a room literally made for pictures: The cabinet-work extends only three feet above the champagne carpeting, leaving the white walls open for a dazzling array of modern art, interspersed with Chinese and Spanish sculpture. It is a room of superb taste and refinement that is also tremendously inviting for all social occasions.

Vast picture windows accentuate the open spaciousness of Kirk Douglas' rambling mansion, as seen from the carved bar and the inner court (below) with its mammoth swimming pool and flagstone deck.

A Rouault and an early
Vlaminck are proudly displayed
in Kirk Douglas's white and
beige living room (above), and a
statue by Ratmir Stojadinovic
graces the garden beyond. Black
and gray, the tones of the travertine
chimney, dominate the den (right)
in which Mrs. Douglas is seated,
while the combination playroom
and projection room is paneled
in walnut (above, right).

154

Henry Fonda's Bel-Air home—a combination of Spanish traditional and modern architectures. Flagstone steps lead down from an open patio to a pool flanked by nineteenth-century French statuary (below, left). In the comfortable den and library designed by Peter Shore, Mr. and Mrs. Fonda are surrounded by many of their favorite paintings (below).
Overleaf:
The Fonda living room—elegance without ostentation, rugged yet rich in its effect.

A gallery in the Fonda home (left and above) contains one of Mr. Fonda's own paintings. An artist of considerable talent, he has several of his canvases on display in the house. For a moment of relaxation, he shoots a round of pool with designer Peter Shore (top).

The hilltop home that publicist Rupert Allen shares with film-producer Brigadier General Frank McCarthy was built upon the tennis court of the former John Barrymore estate. The picture windows in the living room (right) command a breathtaking view of Los Angeles.

Actually two houses with a shared patio, pool, and living room, they are joined by covered walks lined with art posters. The entrance (left) is through Louis XIV doors flanked by della Robbia medallions of Dante and Beatrice.

Rock Hudson

O NE OF THE more sumptuous bachelor pads in the movie colony is the California-Spanish hilltop home of the handsome Rock Hudson. Built in 1934 and formerly owned by agent Sam Jaffe, the house was rented by Hudson for a number of years, then purchased in 1962; whereupon, with the assistance of noted designer Peter Shore, he launched upon an extended program of redecorating it to his own taste. Today, although Mr. Hudson claims he still has two years to go, the place seems comfortably complete and thoroughly lived-in. Moreover, it is appropriately scaled to his massive 6 foot 4 inch frame.

As in most Spanish-style houses, the focus is upon the patio, in this instance formed by the two arms of the house itself and dominated by a large rectangular swimming pool. At the far end, overlooking a superb view of Beverly Hills, stands a colonnade of eight cast-iron pillars originally part of a Pasadena bank; four large antique Italian statues of lions stand guard at each corner of the pool. For parties, the pool is covered over and converted into a dance floor, the columns providing a background for the orchestra. Between the pool and the arches leading to the house, a graceful Chinese elm casts its shade over a broad, flagstoned open area.

Although the rooms are spacious, there are surprisingly few of them for a house north ends of the house look out upon a great rolling lawn sloping down to a dark

its size. The downstairs consists of a large, formal living room, a large den, dining room, kitchen, and a small guest-bedroom opening off the patio; the second story contains only the master suite and another guest room. Perhaps the most impressive of these is the rather Italianate living room, in which even Mr. Hudson's grand piano, topped by a giant spray of orchids and a soaring, wood-carved eagle, seems dwarfed. At the far end, opposite broad, white plaster arches based in raw stone, rises a handsome Italian Renaissance marble fireplace from San Marino, flanked by deep, velvet-covered couches, behind one of which lurks a superbly detailed stone lion from Ethiopia. Symptomatic of the tasteful eclecticism that characterizes all the furnishings, the room includes both an elaborately carved *prie-dieu* purchased from the Hearst collection at San Simeon and also, prominently displayed between two massive wing chairs covered in a specially woven black, gold, and red tapestry, a green marble bust that Mr. Hudson discovered in a junk shop. The room is kept decorated with a profusion of flowers and plants.

As might be expected, the den is considerably more intimate and also more rugged, with much wood set against the bare white walls, and further set off by a red and black Spanish rug. One wall is completely lined with Rock Hudson's hi-fi phonograph, stereo tuner, and record collection, supported on raw planks that once were painters' scaffolds. These in turn rest on antique wooden corbels acquired from San Simeon. A great sprawling couch with leopard-skin cushions has been set against one wall, with a hand-hewn Spanish coffee table topped in tooled leather in front of it. Wood panels from sixteenth-century Italian doors complete the room.

The master suite above is dominated by a huge Louis XIII four-poster bed especially made to accommodate the king-size Mr. Hudson. (At the push of a button, incidentally, the head raises up so that its occupant can view the television set, normally concealed behind panels on a bookshelf at the far end of the room.) The wall to the right, which includes a brick wood-burning fireplace, is covered with primitive paintings of nautical subjects, since boats are a particular hobby of Mr. Hudson's. The nautical motif is continued in the lamps about the room, fashioned from ships' fittings. The room also contains many of the statues and plaques that he has been awarded over the years—most notably, the German "Bambis" as "most popular actor." In the dressing room just beyond, the large dresser has been created out of a bacon rack from Ireland. And thanks to the splendid isolation of his home, the shower has a glass wall that affords a panoramic view of the canyon below.

Somewhat more formal is the guest room on the second floor, with its dark paneled door and recessed wood-paneled wall with built-in sofa, surmounted by the bronze bust of a laughing satyr. The remaining walls are covered in red cut-velvet, broken by a splendid antique armoire from Austria and numerous prints and paintings—including one of the *Khairuzan*, a forty-foot ketch rig yacht that was Mr. Hudson's special joy until the pressures of a global picture schedule made its continued maintenance impractical. The large bed is covered by a solid-red throw of pure vicuna. Just off this room a smaller one has been outfitted with the latest in hi-fi equipment, including a console on which Mr. Hudson can record or mix tape tracks to his satisfaction.

"What I had in mind for Rock," said Mr. Shore, "is a place that would be comfortable and relaxing—a home, not a set." Rock Hudson would be the first to agree that that is precisely what he has gotten.

An antique Italian lion—one of four—stands guard over Rock Hudson's patio swimming pool.

Rock Hudson's den (above) skillfully combines rough wood, such as the painters' scaffolds that serve as record shelves, with fine leather, such as the richly tooled surface of the Spanish coffee table. At right, Mr. Hudson romps with a pet.

The guest room (below) includes
an antique Austrian armoire, red
cut-velvet walls, and a bed throw
of red vicuna. Adjacent to it is
a music room (at bottom) with
hi-fi equipment for recording
and mixing tapes, a hobby of
Mr. Hudson's.

Rock Hudson's bedroom and
living room (next four pages) reflect the grand scale of the entire
house, and also the range of its
owner's enthusiasms—a fondness
for boating and a passion for
music.

Bobby Darin, Richard Crenna, Jeffrey Hayden and Eva Marie Saint

OR MOST Hollywood personalities on the rise, a home in Beverly Hills (particularly in the block just north of Sunset Boulevard) seems the ultimate proof of arrival. Its broad, curving, palm-lined streets, scoured of pedestrians by the vigilant Beverly Hills police, bespeak prosperity and security, two attributes particularly prized by the laborers in movieland's volatile vineyards. Further reassurance derives from the fact that, in Beverly Hills, one's neighbors tend to be one's peers—a famous star on the right, a noted director on the left, and the head of a large studio just across the street. And oddly enough, in Beverly Hills neighbors actually are neighbors. Although the homes are often quite large, with extensive grounds in the back for gardens, swimming pools and tennis courts, the frontages are relatively restricted; the houses, virtually filling their lots, are brought into close proximity to each other. Many an ambitious newcomer has moved into Beverly Hills more for the neighbors than the neighborhood.

By the same token, there is considerable mobility in the Beverly Hills home market. As careers rise, fall or alter, owners tend to look for larger or smaller quarters, or even depart Beverly Hills altogether. Symptomatically, less than a year after the photographs of Bobby Darin's luxurious bachelor pad were taken for this folio, Darin had moved on. His career in films frequently took him to distant locations, and personal appearances on concert tours and in supper clubs also kept him away from home for extended periods. At publication time, the trim tan and black structure in the very heart of Beverly Hills was up for sale, while Darin hunted a smaller, more relaxing place in Malibu.

There are others who tend to shy away from Beverly Hills for the very reason that they prefer to avoid the propinquity of neighbors; they like the privacy and spaciousness of the hills and canyons. One such is director Jeffrey Hayden and his lovely actress wife, Eva Marie Saint. With their two children, Darrell and Laurette, they have been living since 1958 in a sprawling ranch-style home that, surrounded by towering California sycamores, nestles in the lower reaches of Mandeville Canyon (which is fast becoming the Wilton of the West—an exurbanite colony of successful artists seeking to preserve their own identity).

An ivy fence, a broad lawn and a stream separate the Hayden home, yellow with white trim under a heavy shake roof, from the canyon's main road. A long one-story wooden structure with a large overhang on the canyon side, it is bisected by a covered breezeway that effectively divides the living areas—living room, dining room, den and bedrooms—from Mr. Hayden's office and the adjacent "studio room" that is used on a first-come, first-served basis for children's games, Mrs. Hayden's sewing or painting and, on occasion, for movie shows. (The 16mm projector is set up in an adjoining closet with special ports cut into the wall.) Most of the rooms open directly onto a large patio behind the house which in turn leads to a huge playground extending back to the mountains.

Inside, the predominant color scheme is pale greens and beige, accented with panelings of warm woods. The large, airy living room, for example, has two walls finished in a light green plaster, a third wall and alcove is finished in oak, and at the far end, floor-to-ceiling drapes of pale beige diffuse the light from picture windows. Two large davenports are upholstered in a darker green, and the nubbled wall-to-wall carpeting is a still darker shade. Furnishings follow no particular style: Graceful and authentic bentwood chairs may be placed near the hard lines of a contemporary Scandinavian coffee table. Their pieces, as Jeffrey Hayden readily explains, have been collected by both of them over the years and assembled into rooms that are large enough and neutral enough to display each to advantage.

Like many young Californians, the Haydens are also avid art collectors, specializing in the works of California artists. Paintings by Billy Brice, Bill Brown, Frank Stella and James Weeks hang throughout the house, while in the living room a large James Strombotne is displayed over one davenport and, almost filling the wall beyond the piano, an even larger canvas by Paul Wonner. But the place of honor, centered over the mantel shelf in the living room, goes to a delicate watercolor by Andrew Wyeth. Altogether, it is a house that reflects with charming informality the tastes and enthusiasms of its two gifted occupants.

With the proliferation of freeways in the Fifties and Sixties, and the increasing concentration of studios in San Fernando Valley, older, formerly rather inaccessible Valley communities like Thousand Oaks, Sherman Oaks and Encino began to attract the movie colony and—since television production tended to center in the Valley—the TV crowd as well. Some moved into new hillside tracts bulldozed out of the northern slopes of the Santa Monica Mountains (with Beverly Hills and Bel-Air just over the ridge), while others, like actor Richard Crenna, sought out older houses and remodeled them to suit their own needs and desires.

The Crenna home—shared by wife Tenni, three children, two cats, and a large Collie named Missy—is a large, rambling place surrounded by birch trees, silk oaks and dollar eucalyptus. At an 1,100-foot elevation, it commands an impressive view of San Fernando Valley, while trees screen it off from still higher neighbors. Built about thirty years ago, its exterior was a depressing dark brown when Crenna acquired it in 1965, and its interior was crammed with horrendous Western trophies. Today, the single-story house is spanking white under its brown shake roof, with a mustard trim for the windows and doors. Ivy vines and camellia trees lend grace to its walls.

Inside, the home has much the feeling of a French country house, particularly since the furniture runs to French and Italian provincial. Mrs. Crenna, an interior decorator, loves to pick up odd and attractive pieces when her husband is working on location, however—Chinese vases and aborigine weavings, for example, are among the booty from almost a year in Taiwan during the filming of *The Sand Pebbles*—and these are stored in the three-car garage (with no room left for the cars) until an advantageous place is found for them in the house. "The Crenna Instant Decorating Service," Dick Crenna wryly calls his garage, for he also uses it as a workshop for anything that needs building or repairing around the house. A badminton court, a *bocce* alley, a tree house, a fruit orchard and a swimming pool with separate pool house complete the property. Or almost. Currently in construction is a two-story addition that will provide two extra bedrooms. The Crennas like to come together at mealtime in their large combination dining room and kitchen; apart from that, Mr. Crenna feels, "Everyone should have his own place to go."

Overleaf:
Singer Bobby Darin's Beverly Hills bachelor pad.

So far as any house can be called typical of Beverly Hills, Bobby Darin's recent home (above) fits the description—stucco walls, Spanish-tiled roof, a broad driveway for off-street parking. Typical too is the wood-paneled game room with its championship pool table.

Beyond Beverly Hills and Bel-Air, just before the Pacific Palisades, lies rugged, beautiful Mandeville Canyon, increasingly popular with the movie colony. At right is the spacious, tree-shaded home of actress Eva Marie Saint and her director-husband, Jeffrey Hayden.

Thanks to Los Angeles'
ever-expanding freeway
system, San Fernando
Valley has become the newest
studio center, and many film
and TV personalities now
swear they would live nowhere
else—among them actor
Richard Crenna, who has
completely remodeled this old
Encino mansion.

Joe Hyams and Elke Sommer, Mel Shavelson, Delmer Daves

 OR MOST PEOPLE, a home is merely a place to live—a place to entertain and to relax in. For some, the home is also a place to do the work that takes one's mind off working—a place to ride a favorite hobby horse in any direction that strikes the fancy. In Hollywood, no doubt, there are those who follow the more conventional hobbies, like stamp collecting or bird watching; but as with everything else about the movies, even the hobbies of the film people tend to be on a larger-than-life scale. Instead of collecting stamps, one actor collects vintage motorcars. Another, with a taste for modern art, has transformed his home into a veritable museum. And a true hi-fi enthusiast is not at all averse to remodeling an entire house if it will improve the acoustics.

The fact is that movie people have the money and, when not actually in production, the time to indulge their fancies; and many of their homes have either been purchased or built with an eye to accommodating them. For actress Elke Sommer, married to writer and former columnist Joe Hyams, the hobby is painting; and much of the life in their huge home in the Holmby Hills actually centers about a much smaller guest house on the property because it includes the den in which Miss Sommer paints while her husband types. It is a large, sunny, lofted room with white walls and a high ceiling beamed with dark walnut. In an alcove at one end, his back to the garden and pool, Mr. Hyams has installed his desk, its top fashioned from two oak doors.

If the view behind him might be distracting to a writer, the view to the front could only be more so, for at the opposite end of the room is Elke Sommer's studio. Here, working at a large easel or, more often, crouching over a canvas spread flat on the floor, the beauteous Miss Sommer creates pictures that have been exhibited in Los Angeles' McKenzie Gallery, the California Museum of Science and Industry, and in several European museums. In addition, almost all the pictures in their home are ones that she herself has painted.

The main house, designed by architect Paul Williams, is English Colonial and built on a baronial scale. Its living room and den—light green walls spackled with brown—extends over eighty feet. Its vast dining room, built around a long, oval oak table and magnificent pewter chandelier, can seat eighteen guests comfortably. Furnishings are an eye-pleasing medley of pieces acquired all over the world—from Germany, Spain and, most recently, from Iran, while Miss Sommer was filming *The Heroes*. Surprisingly, for all its vastness the house has only two bedrooms.

For producer-writer-director Mel Shavelson, the hobby is ham radio, and he operates his two-kilowatt, single side-band transmitter W6VLH from a large, paneled room at the far end of his graceful, rambling California Colonial home.

Complete with radio teletype and automated tape, his set puts him in two-way voice communication with every continent on the globe—and with scientific expeditions at the South Pole as well. Work schedule permitting, he is customarily at his microphone for an hour or so before breakfast, although frequently, like most ham operators, he sets up "phone patches" connecting members of the Peace Corps or the armed services with their folks back home.

The Shavelsons have lived in their Studio City home since 1953. Set well back from a quiet road leading into Laurel Canyon, the low, one-story red brick and plaster building is reached through a tree-lined blacktop that curves down to a large carport and turn-around area. The path to the main entrance leads past scrupulously tended flower beds that seem in full bloom at every season. Beyond the house lie a superb rose garden, a croquet lawn and an orchard. To the rear, reached by a large brick patio, rolling lawns stretch away to a king-sized swimming pool and, to the left, a championship tennis court. Next to radio, tennis is Mel Shavelson's favorite sport; both he and his wife, Lucy, are ardent and expert players.

They are also ardent and attentive hosts. Several times during a year their lawn might become the scene of a fund-raising charity event, or their large early-American living room the center for a serious celebrity-studded discussion of current affairs. Adding to the pleasure of such occasions is the adjoining wood-lined playroom with its comfortable conversational groupings and, at one end, a combination bar and soda fountain that dispenses everything from malted milks to draft beer, not to mention the more spirituous beverages. A large closet off the room conceals 35mm projection equipment, ready for instant use through a port behind the bar.

An annual event at the Shavelsons is their New Year's Day "Hangover Party," to which literally hundreds of their friends are bussed (thus avoiding parking problems) to watch the Rose Bowl game on three color television sets and to get over the night before. The parties for 1968 and 1969 had to be canceled, however. As Shavelson wrote to his friends: "1968—Flew to Hong Kong. 1969—Hong Kong flu to us. Velly solly."

Mineralogy and etymology are producer-writer-director Delmer Daves' most persistent hobbies. One collection of his rare, semiprecious stones has already gone to Stanford University and another is in the process of building. An avid reader, he has made himself an authority not only on minerals but on the geographies that produce them, and on the arts, architectures and costumes of the world. Everything that is pertinent is systematically clipped and filed away in folders that are carefully, uniquely labeled and cross-referenced in a manner that would do credit to a trained librarian. At this point, his clipping files alone almost fill a sizable room; as a folder becomes full, its contents are removed to boxes that now line the room from floor to ceiling. In the adjacent room, a wood-paneled study, his mineral collection is handled with similar skill and finesse, the rock samples displayed in drawers set into special cabinets. A twenty-five-year interest in etymology accounts for the horde of dictionaries and reference works that fill the study's built-in shelves, broken only by sketches and lithographs, many of them by the protean Mr. Daves.

Indeed, before Daves and his actress wife, Mary Lawrence, could even move into their Bel-Air home back in 1939, they had to wait until a separate building was completed to house the collections that had already begun accumulating. The house itself, a stately Southern Colonial mansion with New Orleans-style grillwork on its façade, is distinguished by large and gracious rooms, a vast terraced patio in the rear (often used for cook-outs and informal entertaining), and great stretches of neatly tended lawn and garden. For Mrs. Daves, the special favorite is her Portuguese blue bedroom, its textiled walls matching the color and design of the drapes and throws. For Mr. Daves, of course, the favorite is his comfortable study, with all of his hobbies just a few steps away.

Overleaf:
As talented as she is decorative, Miss Sommer loves to paint at home—with happy results. She has had several one-man (or -woman) shows, and her work is now in numerous collections.

Elke Sommer, surrounded by her own paintings, entertains in the eighty-foot living room of her Holmby Hills mansion (left). The guest house (above) is her studio, an alcove of which is also the office of her writer husband, Joe Hyams (below). Guest rooms open off the loft on the second floor.

Hobbies—often expensive hobbies—are also a part of the Hollywood way of life. Producer-writer-director Mel Shavelson is a licensed ham radio operator and has converted an entire room of his valley home into a studio. An annual event at the Shavelsons' is the New Year's Day football telecast, with hundreds of celebrated friends as absorbed spectators.

*Producer-director-writer
Delmer Daves is also an ardent
collector. In a separate building of
his Beverly Hills estate he keeps
research files and books on art,
geography, history, and—his
special passion—mineralogy.
Many of the graphics in this
studio were created by Daves himself.*

Charlton Heston, Jennings Lang, Taft Schrieber

SOUTHERN CALIFORNIA sunshine and its mountainous terrain has produced a style of architecture that is no less distinctive. New homes often incorporate the native multicolored flagstones and hardwoods. Cantilevered construction has become more the rule than the exception, particularly for hillside houses. And to capitalize on the views and vistas from the heights, entire walls are often simply great sheets of glass, with supports for the roof reduced to narrow strips of structural steel that afford a minimal obstruction and maximal strength. Even on the flatlands below the mountains, the picture window has become almost *de rigueur*, with exuberant plantings and sculpture gardens providing the picture. If white stucco was once the typical building material of the area, it has long since been supplanted by plate glass.

Exemplifying much of this is the star-shaped hilltop house that the late Welton Beckett designed for Charlton Heston in 1958. Heston refers to it as "the house *Ben Hur* built," for he was off making that picture during most of its construction; he and his family moved into it in 1960. His own description of its style is "Medieval Modern." Built of stone, steel and glass, and overlooking the whole of Hidden Valley from the brow of the Santa Monica Mountains, it occupies, in Mr. Heston's words, "a superb defensive position, which is an ideal spot for an actor to be in." Its colors, both inside and out, derive from the stone from which it was constructed —beiges, browns and grays.

Essentially, the design of the house is two intersecting triangles, with a large, cypress-lined garden forming the hypotenuse of the larger. At one end, an impressive *galleria* looks out through floor-to-ceiling windows toward its series of fountains and reflecting pool. The *galleria* itself is dominated by a huge lantern of polished brass, originally created for Douglas Fairbanks' *The Thief of Bagdad*. (Another, even larger, hangs in the living room.) On a false wall especially constructed for the purpose is displayed a Piranese canvas, *The Tomb of Cecelia Metella*; it holds a special significance for the Hestons since the tomb itself was not far from their home during the filming of *Ben Hur*.

Like Charlton Heston, everything about the house is on the grand scale. Although, apart from the two-story kitchen wing, it is entirely on a single level, the ceilings are high—anywhere from fourteen feet in his glassed-in den to a soaring twenty feet in the *galleria*. In the master bedroom, Mrs. Heston alone has forty-four running feet of closet space. The den, which is also Mr. Heston's workroom, features an extra-large desk created for him by his actor friend Milburn Stone. And outside the den, cantilevered over Hidden Valley, a hardwood sun deck affords generous space for relaxation. In its totality, the effect of the house is sunny, open, and unostentatiously but indisputably modern.

The same is true of television executive Jennings Lang's handsome Beverly Hills home, although when it was built for producer Pandro Berman its style was Georgian traditional. During more than two years of remodeling, the house was made to look more contemporary on the outside by painting the woodwork white above the first story's red brick, and on the inside by opening up rooms, by installations of floor-to-ceiling cabinetwork, and by lavish applications of modern art. In the vast entryway, open to the entire height of the house, a huge canvas by Billy Brice all but dwarfs its graceful chandelier. An ingeniously mobile stone sculpture by Cascella and a large piece by Sorel Etrog (whose work is represented a number of times in the Langs' collection) admirably set the tone of what is to follow.

Directly ahead is the library, with its malachite green rug and easy chairs; blond wood paneling conceals bookshelves, a bar and a TV set (one of nineteen strategically placed about the house). The large living room, which houses a fine collection of pre-Colombian pieces, also doubles as a projection room: The panel containing a large Alishinsky, *The Innocent Children*, slides down to reveal the projector ports. The room's gold and green decor affords a rich setting for a charming small sculpture by Miró, a large marble by Etrog and, set into a window seat, a handsome copper sphere by Pomedoro. In a large closet to one side, Mrs. Lang (actress and singer Monica Lewis) stores an extensive record collection and her hi-fi equipment.

But the quintessence of the Jennings Lang house is not to be found in the house itself, but rather in the pool house that they themselves built upon the estate. Although the red brick and white wood trim reflect the basic style of the main building, floor-to-ceiling sliding glass doors and glass walls add the distinctively modern note, as do the black concrete and brick floors and the white plaster walls hung with colorful Haitian primitives. It looks out over a large pool and, below that, a superb green tennis court (with its own dressing pavillion) and, to the other side, a beautifully terraced and carefully tended garden shaded by a 200-year = old live oak. Swinging plastic squares designed by Koschie, a large marble by Etrog, and a nine-foot bronze by Michael Ayerton, *Lady in Hammock*, are among the works artfully displayed in the open air.

Perhaps the finest sculpture garden in Beverly Hills, however—if not, indeed, in all of Southern California—is that belonging to Taft B. Schreiber, a senior executive at MCA. The house itself, built between 1956 and 1958, is in the style that has since become identified as California modern, with great glass-enclosed spaces opening to the sun wherever possible; but since the main life of the house is oriented toward the patio and gardens to the rear, it maintains something of the traditional California Colonial as well. Its walls contain a superb collection of modern art, ranging from Cézanne and Matisse to Braque, Kandinsky and Mondrian, and on to such contemporary painters as Jackson Pollock and Willem de Kooning.

But even more impressive are the works in the garden. Two gaunt Giacometti women, almost as tall as the house itself, stand just outside the glass-enclosed back porch. Beyond the porch, in an open patio from which hangs George Rickey's delicate *Nuages*, stand the Cubist *Man and Guitar*, an early work by Jacques Lipschitz. In the gardens, flanking the pool, is a masterful *Mother and Child* by Henry Moore and a stabile by Alexander Calder. Also in the gardens are a new stabile-mobile created by Calder specifically for Mr. Schreiber, a two-piece Henry Moore, *Reclining Figure*, and many more. Altogether, it is a collection that any museum might well envy.

California modern is the style of actor Charlton Heston's spectacular hilltop home, where
floor-to-ceiling windows bring the out-of-doors into every room

Off the master bedroom, a tile-
lined steam room (above) proves
an ideal place to relax. And
from the cantilevered sun deck outside his den, Charlton Heston
can gaze out over Hidden Valley
(right). The swimming pool
and an outdoor gym are marked
by the cypress trees.

MCA executive Jennings Lang
and wife, singer Monica Lewis,
entertain friends on the patio
of the pool house of their Beverly
Hills estate (above). The
interior of the pool house (right)
features a Lucio carving over the
fireplace—and a TV set in
the armoire.

A Sunday morning on the Lang. tennis court (below). On a terrace well below the house, it is reached through an extensive sculpture garden that includes Michael Ayerton's nine-foot bronze "Lady in Hammock." Even the ropes of the hammock are bronze.

Overleaf: MCA executive Taft Schreiber's sculpture garden is dominated by Henry Moore's "Mother and Child."

Beneath metallic clouds created
by George Rickey, the Schreibers'
garden patio (above, left) includes an important Negri and
Jacques Lipchitz' cubist "Man
and Guitar" (seen in closer
view, left, below). In the sculpture
garden a Calder stabile stands
beside the swimming pool,
opposite Moore's "Mother and
Child." Moore's two-piece
"Reclining Figure" (left) is also
featured in this remarkable
collection.

Two towering Giacometti female
figures stand outside the glass-
enclosed patio of Taft Schreiber's
California modern home as
seen from outside and within
(above).

William AND Edith Goetz

HOUSING ONE of the great privately owned French Impressionist collections in the United States is the two-story mansion of former producer William Goetz (now a banker) and his diminutive, attractive wife, Edith, daughter of the fabled Louis B. Mayer. Located in the very heart of fashionable Bel-Air, the Goetzes' home today perhaps most closely approximates the position held by Pickfair during the Twenties as a center of the film community's social and political life. At the Goetzes' renowned parties movie stars mingle with political leaders, educators, and artists; an intimate dinner may be set for a dozen or more guests. The lavish way of life for which Hollywood was once justly noted still continues here, undiminished in zest—although undoubtedly more refined in spirit.

The approach to the house, which was built in the early Forties, is past a large box-hedged motor court that leads to a wrought-iron porte cochère. Latticed shutters lend the dove-gray exterior a rather austere look, but this is belied as soon as one steps inside the long reception hall, which is in fact a gallery of modern art. Along its pale-pink walls hang choice canvasses by such Impressionists as Bonnard, Cézanne, Monet, Renoir, and Toulouse-Lautrec, as well as an outstanding collection of Fauvist paintings. The floors of this impressive hall—and, indeed, of the entire main floor—are of gleaming, polished parquet, with large area-rugs to match the decor of the various rooms.

To the right of the entrance is a small (by Goetz standards) wood-paneled, book-lined room—the library—whose comfortable chairs afford a relaxed intimacy for a business conversation or for a companionable drink from its bar. Dominating the library, a large Van Gogh self-portrait glares out from above the low fireplace. Beyond the far wall, reached by a broad, open archway, stands an airy, semicircular library bay, used primarily for business purposes. Through its windows one catches a partial glimpse of the rolling, parklike lawns and gardens to the rear of the house. It is here, on the scrupulously manicured lawn, beyond a green and white canopy that extends some sixty feet across the central portion of the rear façade, that Mrs. Goetz gives large fund-raising parties for the numerous charities she is interested in. (Her formal parties, however, are always held inside.)

Particularly attractive is the semienclosed area beneath the canopy, designed and decorated by Mrs. Laura Mako. It is a deep, long porch with a terrazzo floor, furnished with broad, inviting bamboo sofas and chairs. Potted ferns and giant-leafed *monstera* create a sense of indoor-outdoor living.

But the center of the house is its vast, majestic, yet gracious living room. Lined on one side with great windows looking out toward the garden, flanked by pale aqua-blue drapes that reach from ceiling to floor, it is a room designed for entertaining. Potted plants and bowls of flowers, set upon low tortoiseshell tables placed among comfortably upholstered chairs and sofas covered in whites and yellows, continue the indoor-outdoor motif. Color accents come from the blue porcelain Lowestoft lamp bases and from blue-, brown-, and champagne-colored cushions scattered about the furniture. Once again the walls, a pale aqua-blue, are hung with great paintings by the French Impressionists, and a number of glass-covered cabinets display priceless figurines from China's Ming and T'ang eras.

Because museums are constantly borrowing pictures in the Goetz collection, repeated visits to the house have something of the effect of returning to a gallery that frequently changes its exhibitions. (On one recent occasion so many of their favorite pictures were gone from the walls that the Goetzes decided to take a vacation until at least some of them had returned.) But there are three especially prized paintings—a Monet, a Toulouse-Lautrec, and a Sisley—that never leave their places. These are bolted firmly to a wall panel that lifts up at the flip of a switch, to reveal a projection booth equipped with two theatrical-standard 35mm sound projectors. Another switch lowers a movie screen at the far side of the room; and still another converts two small cabinets on either side of it, ordinarily used to display Chinese *objets d'art*, into loudspeakers. The furniture is arranged so that everyone has a perfect view of the screen.

Beyond the living room is the sumptuously proportioned dining room, with its great golden candelabra, its enormous, dark-mahogany, eighteenth-century Sheraton table (it can seat up to twenty-four), and its mahogany, yellow-velvet-cushioned chairs. Its white walls are broken only by two ceiling-to-floor yellow silk serge curtains at the windows, with a magnificent Bonnard—Mrs. Goetz's favorite—between them. A Degas hangs against a baffle at the far end of the room which conceals the service area, and in a bay at the opposite end a large tortoiseshell table can accommodate another dozen guests. The service is silver, the tear-drop crystal from Scotland, and the food, always prepared under Mrs. Goetz's personal supervision, is never less than Lucullan. The room, originally decorated by William Haines, has recently been redone by Mrs. Mako, as have parts of the living room.

The Goetz house, which has long enjoyed a reputation for its gracious entertaining, deserves more than that: It sets a glowing standard for gracious living.

One of the most palatial of the newer Beverly Hills mansions, the home of financier and former producer William Goetz is a focal point of movie-colony social and cultural activity. The magnificent semienclosed rear patio, with its striped canopy, looks out over more than an acre of rolling lawn.

*Mrs. Edith Goetz in her
favorite sitting room (above),
with a Van Gogh self-portrait on
the wall and semicircular
library beyond.*

The dining room (above) set
with silver service for eighteen.
Paintings by Bonnard and
Degas adorn the walls. The living
room (below, left and right) is a
veritable gallery of Impressionist
painting—but at the touch of a
button it converts into a movie
theater as wall panel lifts up
to reveal projectors.

Overleaf:
The Goetz living room, designed
by Mrs. Laura Mako, with
glimpse of patio beyond.

James Coburn
Steve McQueen

TWO OF HOLLYWOOD'S fastest-rising stars are James Coburn and Steve McQueen, and, symbolic of their status, both have moved into palatial homes—Coburn in Beverly Hills, McQueen farther west in Brentwood—which they then proceeded to decorate to their own tastes and inclinations. For Mr. Coburn and his wife, Beverly, the problem was more than simple decoration. The 2½-acre estate that they purchased in 1964 from George Kolb, scion of a Philadelphia baking family, included such details as a green-cobbled court filled with large concrete statues. Although the Coburns did little to the house structurally, they found it necessary to strip both the inside and the exterior completely before they could proceed with their own decorating plans.

Because the house, with its white stucco walls, Spanish-tiled roof, and rounded turrets, is decidedly Mediterranean—even somewhat Moorish—in appearance, they chose this to provide a unifying motif to the interior decor. The Moors, as Mrs. Coburn explains, provided a bridge between the Mediterranean cultures and the Far East, and hence carefully selected pieces from as far off as Thailand and Japan can be artfully mingled with fabrics and furnishings from Italy, Spain, and by extension, Mexico. As designed by noted art-director and decorator Tony Duquette (with an occasional assist from Coburn himself, who loves to rummage about for unique treasures when filming in distant lands), this theory has produced a home that is at once distinctive, original, and harmonious.

One immediately notes the Moorish flavor upon stepping into the large octagonal entry hall with its shallow tiled basin, out of which grow graceful sprays of moth orchids. Tiled panels (from the original house) flank the curtained archways leading off to other rooms, and eight lamps hung from the mirrored ceiling with delicate strands of crystal surround a great mirrored globe from which descend more crystal strands, almost touching the flowers. Particularly notable is the use of mirrors throughout the house—on walls, on ceilings—to enhance the symmetry of the rooms, to augment the sense of spaciousness and light, and also to provide a feeling of flow from one room to the next.

The center of the house is the huge living room, which seems to radiate from a stylized Mexican sun-mirror, created by Duquette out of gilded plaster and bird-of-paradise feathers, centered in its far wall. Above it the ceiling beams have been encrusted with translucent shells and gilded in a rattan pattern; the tone of the ceiling, covered in a textured blue material, is continued in the almost ceiling-to-floor curtains at the windows. To the left a stone fireplace, almost as tall as a man, is flanked by elaborate candelabra fashioned from Siamese headdresses; and two antique statues of deer, also from Siam, stand nearby. The extensive areas of white, bare walls, according to Mr. Coburn, lend themselves ideally to the presentation of light shows for their guests. Altogether, a swinging house.

On the other hand, Steve McQueen's home, a great stone combination of Mediter-

High on a flowered hill, the Mediterranean-style home of actor James Coburn.

ranean, modern, and ranch, is quite staid and obviously devoted more to creature comforts than to exuberant design. The grounds, for example, have not been altered at all since he purchased the place, save to add electric devices for the protection of his children. But the interiors, created by designer Peter Shore in close collaboration with Mrs. McQueen, the former actress and dancer Neile Adams, have been thoroughly redone—in part to accommodate furniture from the McQueens' earlier home (which Shore also decorated), in part to take full advantage of the greater space in the new one.

The two-story, balconied house is reached by an extended drive winding up through a heavily wooded area that ends in a vast, cobbled motor court. Stone arches shield the house itself from the California sun on the court side, and on the other, a broad, flagstoned patio looks out toward the Pacific, with terraced steps leading down to the sunken garden and the pool. The flagstone continues into the interior of the house—white waxed flagstone in the cozy sitting room, red in the large living room that, thanks to a champion-sized pool table, doubles as a game room as well. Its far wall, in rough stone, is dominated by the flaring horns of a water buffalo set over the fireplace. Several of the comfortable, roomy chairs are covered in animal hides, the whole producing a mixture of textures, styles, and periods which has an oddly agreeable, homey effect.

Upstairs the master bedroom is considerably more formal. The king-size bed, with its tapering, exuberantly carved wooden headboard, is covered by a huge throw of Siberian raccoon, flanked on either side by pendant, Spanish-style lanterns; on the right hang three semiabstract Turkish paintings purchased by Mr. McQueen in London. Beyond the bed, but unified by the brown wall-to-wall carpeting, a small sitting area has been clustered about a marble fireplace. Above it hangs a splendid Spanish lamp of leaded stained-glass, into the base of which Mr. Shore worked a small spotlight that provides illumination either for working or for dining. Off to one side of the bedroom, very feminine in its combination of grays, yellows, orange, and rose, is Mrs. McQueen's dressing room and bath. To the other side, down a short passageway, is Steve McQueen's office, finished in rough woods and with a bearskin on the floor.

It is at once a warm house and a rugged house, a house for play as well as for show, a house for gracious entertaining as well as for intense privacy. The marvel is that it all comes together so agreeably into a house for living.

A Far Eastern motif, designed by Tony Duquette for the Coburns' living room. The broad white walls are often used for light shows.

Overleaf:
Glass and tile create an iridescent effect in the Coburns' entryway, where a mirrored ceiling and mirrors placed in archways augment the sense of space and flow. Iridescent, too, is the crystal chandelier with revolving globe which hangs in the circular stairwell.

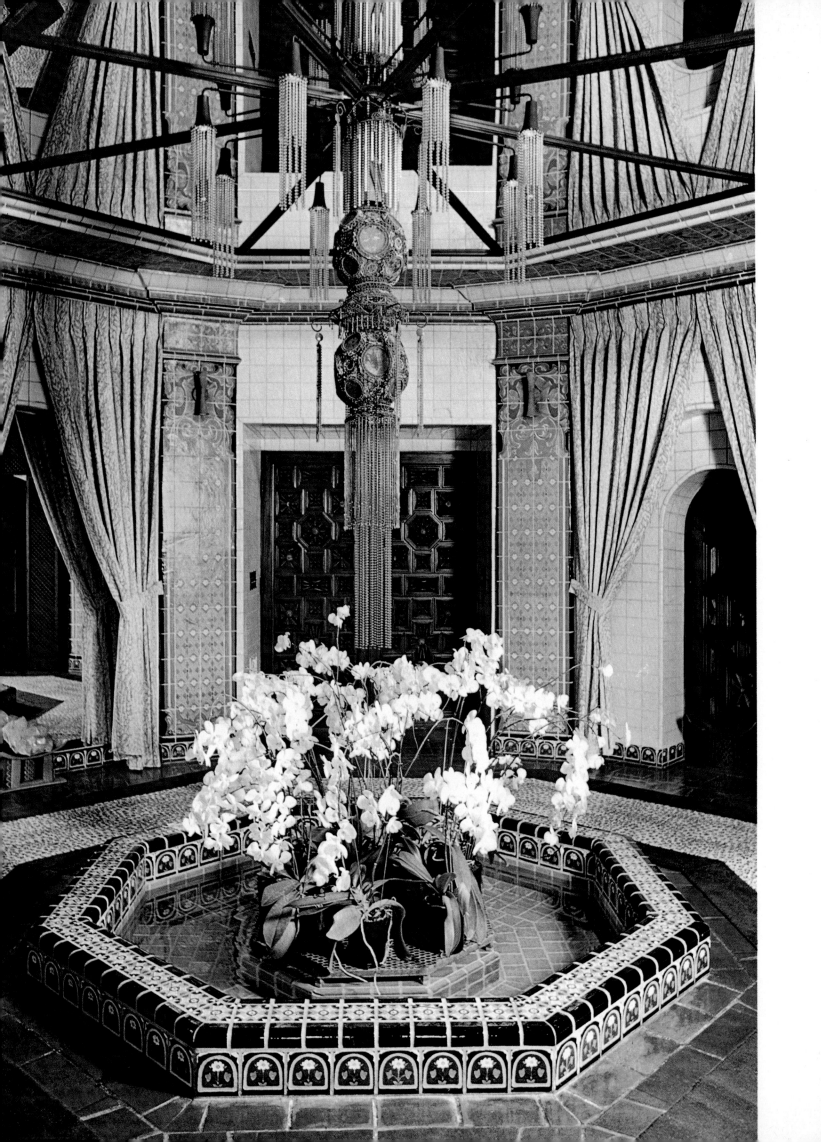

In isolated splendor, the handsome ranch-style house of actor
Steve McQueen looks out toward the distant Pacific. Designed by Peter Shore, the living
room is informal and comfortable
(above), and the master bedroom
(below) displays a richness of
carved woods, fine furs, and
rare paintings.

The McQueens' pool, looking
toward the terrace and house.
It epitomizes the southern
California ideal of healthful,
graceful, comfortable outdoor
living.

A playhouse for the McQueen
children stands in one corner of the
extensive grounds (right). A
broad terrace of flagstone steps
(above) leads down to the pool
area. So high is the house that from
the top of the terrace one has the
impression that below is a sheer
drop of thousands of feet.

Overleaf:
Another view of the bedroom
includes the adjacent sitting room.
A spotlight worked into the
base of the leaded glass lantern
provides illumination.